Born at Home

Cultural and Political Dimensions of Maternity Care in the United States

FIRST EDITION

MELISSA CHEYNEY
Oregon State University

WADSWORTH
CENGAGE Learning™

Australia • Brazil • Japan • Korea • Mexico • Singapore • Spain • United Kingdom • United States

WADSWORTH
CENGAGE Learning

Born at Home: Cultural and Political Dimensions of Maternity Care in the United States, First Edition
Melissa Cheyney

Acquisitions Editor: Erin Mitchell

Developmental Editor: John Young

Assistant Editor: Erin Parkins

Editorial Assistant: Pamela Simon

Media Editor: Melanie Cregger

Marketing Manager:
Andrew Keay

Marketing Assistant:
Dimitri Hagnere

Marketing Communications
Manager: Tami Strang

Content Project Management:
Pre-PressPMG

Creative Director: Rob Hugel

Art Director: Caryl Gorska

Print Buyer: Linda Hsu

Rights Acquisitions Account
Manager, Text: Roberta Broyer

Rights Acquisitions Account
Manager, Image: Robyn Young

Production Service:
Pre-PressPMG

Photo Researcher: Pre-PressPMG

Cover Designer: Carole Lawson

Cover Image: Julie James

Compositor: Pre-PressPMG

For product information and
technology assistance, contact us at **Cengage Learning
Customer & Sales Support, 1-800-354-9706.**

For permission to use material from this text or product, submit all requests online at **www.cengage.com/permissions**.
Further permissions questions can be e-mailed to
permissionrequest@cengage.com.

Library of Congress Control Number: 2010920697

ISBN-13: 978-0-495-79366-3

ISBN-10: 0-495-79366-3

Wadsworth
20 Davis Drive
Belmont, CA 94002-3098
USA

Cengage Learning is a leading provider of customized learning solutions with office locations around the globe, including Singapore, the United Kingdom, Australia, Mexico, Brazil, and Japan. Locate your local office at **www.cengage.com/global**.

Cengage Learning products are represented in Canada by Nelson Education, Ltd.

To learn more about Wadsworth visit
www.cengage.com/Wadsworth

Purchase any of our products at your local college store or at our preferred online store **www.CengageBrain.com.**

Contents

About the Series

This series explores the practical applications of anthropology in understanding and addressing problems faced by human societies around the world. Each case study examines an issue of socially recognized importance in the historical, geographical, and cultural context of a particular region of the world while adding comparative analysis to highlight not only the local effects of globalization but also the global dimensions of the issue. The authors write with a readable narrative style and include reference to their own participation, roles, and responsibilities in the communities they study. Their engagement with people goes beyond observation and research, as they explain and sometimes illustrate from personal experience how their work has implications for advocacy, community action, and policy formation. They demonstrate how anthropological investigations can build our knowledge of human societies and at the same time provide the basis for fostering community empowerment, resolving conflicts, and pursuing social justice.

About the Author

Melissa Cheyney is Assistant Professor of Medical Anthropology and Reproductive Biology at Oregon State University in Corvallis, Oregon, and a Licensed Direct-Entry Midwife. She received her PhD from the University of Oregon in 2005 and currently serves on the state of Oregon's governor-appointed Board of Direct-Entry Midwifery. She is also the Director of Research for the Midwives Alliance of North America; the Vice President of Doulas Supporting Teens, a nonprofit organization serving pregnant and parenting teens; and the director of the Reproductive Health Laboratory at Oregon State University. She has been researching, teaching, and attending births since 1999 and is committed to working for a healthier future for mothers and babies. Her current research interests include the effects of state licensure on the safety of out-of-hospital birth, prenatal nutrition counseling for the prevention of pregnancy complications, and the effects of social support on stress mitigation in pregnancy.

About this Case Study

John A. Young, Series Editor

This book gives readers a window into the hidden and, in some places, outlawed world of homebirth midwifery. The author's background as a Certified Professional Midwife and an applied medical anthropologist provides unique insight into the intimate experience of homebirth and support for its superior outcomes as measured by maternal and infant health. Midwives and birthing mothers tell their stories of resistance to technological models of birthing care and the personal empowerment they feel in delivering their own babies without drugs or surgery. They reveal how midwives develop close relationships with their clients throughout pregnancy and birth, using time-tested rituals and low-tech interventions to optimize chances for success. The author explains the positive outcomes of midwifery in terms of its compatibility with evolutionary human biology and shows how the rationale for opposition from obstetricians and hospitals is related to the dominant cultural view that birth is essentially a dangerous and fearful event. Though the divide is formidable, she points the way toward mutual understanding and suggests specific means of collaboration between midwives and physicians. Finally, she narrates her own role in bringing her findings about the cost-effectiveness of homebirth midwifery into the public dialogue through legislative testimony and policy recommendations.

Preface

I am tremendously proud to hereby introduce this gem of a book by my colleague and friend Melissa—best known as Missy—Cheyney to the public, and even prouder that my work in *Birth as an American Rite of Passage* (1992, 2004) was foundational to Missy's in this book. My book was primarily about hospital birth—its rituals and the profound symbolic messages they send. I always intended to go back and do the same kind of in-depth analysis for the rituals of homebirth, and I am delighted to be relieved of that nagging sense of responsibility, for Missy has done that brilliantly here! And she has also used my work on home-to-hospital transport during labor and after birth (Davis-Floyd, 2003) to illuminate her discussion of that thorny issue in these pages, and to present concrete and achievable suggestions for its resolution, based on strategic planning carried out under Missy's guidance through community participation from all parties—obstetricians, nurses, midwives, and women (see Chapter 6). Missy has also expanded Barbara Katz Rothman's and my definitions of the contrasting medical/technocratic and midwifery/holistic models into a much more nuanced approach that takes into full account midwives' differing perspectives on these models and the ways in which midwives constantly work to navigate these models—to make them into a continuum rather than an opposition. I promise you, dear readers, that you will love and find extraordinarily useful Missy's multifaceted approach to understanding contemporary birth and the ways in which she weaves personal stories into her more academic descriptions and analyses.

This book is about women who choose to give birth at home in the United States despite societal beliefs that frame their choice as irresponsible and risky at best, and criminal at worst. Using the lens of biocultural anthropology, Missy situates homebirth midwifery as a political movement where evolved biology, culture, clinical medicine, and unequal relationships of power combine to produce this marginalized, yet growing, maternity care option. *Born at Home* is an extraordinary exploration into the holistic spirit of childbirth. In it, Missy vividly demonstrates that birth is more than a medical event governed by medical belief and tradition—birth is about culture, tradition, ritual, history, science, politics, and, most of all, power.

Born at Home reveals that birth is not just a one-day event, a clinical process reducible to reportable numbers. Birth is a transformative experience that is embodied and forever-remembered by mothers and their families. In lending authority to the voices of the homebirth community, Missy explores why a small minority of women choose homebirth despite continued social critique, ostracism, and a profound lack of infrastructural support for their choices. This book illustrates how giving birth at home is often as much a political statement as a personal choice. It is a collective call from women and midwives for a radical change in the way we treat birthing mothers and babies in the United States.

Born at Home uses an innovative approach that provides exclusive, firsthand insight into the largely hidden world of homebirth in the United States. As a medical anthropologist, Certified Professional Midwife, and homebirth mother herself, the author has gained unprecedented access to women giving birth at home and to the midwives who attend them, even in states where their practice is illegal. Missy's unique position brings a level of depth and intimacy that is unsurpassed, making *Born at Home* a pioneering biocultural ethnography of a little known and deeply misunderstood phenomenon. Using a numbers and narratives approach, her book combines quantitative data on homebirth outcomes with the dynamic stories of homebirth mothers and their midwives. Statistical indicators of maternal and neonatal well-being demonstrate that birth at home with a trained midwife is a viable, safe, and affordable maternity care option. Her findings form a persuasive argument that I hope will be heeded by policymakers. Homebirth midwifery in the United States holds important keys for improving poor maternal and infant health outcomes, as well as for decreasing health disparities for vulnerable populations.

Using the framework of medical anthropology, *Born at Home* provides readers with an inspirational and informative look at the historical development of childbirth and homebirth midwifery in the United States. Situating homebirth in both global and local perspectives, Missy turns a critical lens on mainstream hospital birth as a highly interventive, medicalized, and often impersonal event. *Born at Home* details the ritualistic and communal nature of homebirth, while situating the practices of midwifery care within the long-term context of evolutionary biology. She uses the politically contentious and highly charged discourses around homebirth to show how women's birthing bodies become sites of struggle for power, social norms, moral values, and cultural legitimacy in health and medicine in the United States. The women featured in this book provide an alternative narrative to the discourse of medicalized birth—a narrative that claims homebirth to be both a personal act of empowerment and an act of social resistance.

Born at Home is not just a book—it is an experience. Using an engaging and alluring writing style, the author invites readers to join her on an intimate journey into the diverse world of homebirth midwifery and homebirthing mothers. Fascinating to scholars, convincing to policymakers, and accessible to undergraduate students, *Born at Home* is an exceptional narrative of revolutionary character with the power to change the experiences of an entire generation of birthing women. As you read and discuss this book, may you emerge claiming your own informed right to choose where and with whom you deliver.

–Robbie Davis-Floyd
Austin, Texas
October 2009

A personal note: Thank you, Missy, for bringing my work back home, where I always wanted it to be!

REFERENCES

Davis-Floyd, R. (2003). Home birth emergencies in the U.S. and Mexico: The trouble with transport. In G. Jenkins & M. Ihorn (Eds.), *Reproduction Gone Awry*, a special issue of *Social Science and Medicine, 56*(9): 1913–1931. Also available at www.davis-floyd.com

Davis-Floyd, R. E. (1992/2004). *Birth as an American rite of passage*. Berkeley: University of California Press.

Chapter 1

Midwifery in Cross-Cultural and Historical Perspective

Childbirth is not merely a physiological process; therefore, a biomedical model is insufficient to understand its many dimensions. In the practices of every culture, and in the embodied memories of every birthing woman, including those in North America, childbirth transforms women, babies and their supporters through what many call—perhaps too easily—the "miracle of birth."
—Pamela Klassen, 2001, pp. 218–219

This book is a celebration, a celebration of the birthing body—its biology, its chemistry, its evolution, and, most of all, its power. It gives voice to a marginalized group of women in the United States who choose to deliver their babies at home with midwives and, in doing so, reject the cultural norm of obstetrician-attended hospital birth. I examine the cultural, political, and clinical perspectives of a small yet highly vocal and politically motivated group of birth activists who take direct action to challenge one of the most deeply entrenched assumptions of our time—that the application of medical technologies in the birthplace has substantially improved the well-being of mothers and babies. Through an examination of mothers' birthing narratives, midwives' stories, and birth statistics collected during five years of fieldwork in two cities in the United States, this book explores the lived experiences of homebirthing women and the midwives who care for them.

STUDY BACKGROUND

The majority of high-income nations in the world today, including Germany, the Netherlands, Ireland, England, New Zealand, and the Scandinavian countries, have embraced a public health strategy where trained midwives attend as many as 75 percent of births, and home and birth-center births are widely available for low-risk women (Wagner, 2006). Obstetricians in these systems almost exclusively attend high-risk mothers who require specialized interventions, while midwives offer high-quality, individualized, and lower-cost care to the majority of women. Midwifery-dominated approaches are progressively forming the foundation for maternal and infant health structures around the world because they are associated with lower rates of interventions, improved clinical and psychosocial outcomes, and significant decreases in costs and disparities in access to care.

In light of these benefits, a growing public health focus spearheaded by the World Health Organization and the American Public Health Association point to midwife-attended births, both in- and out-of-hospital, as one option for cutting costs and improving access to birthing care in the United States. *Out-of-hospital* is a term used to refer to births that occur either in a private home or in a home-like, independent birth center, as opposed to a hospital or birth centers on hospital grounds. Proponents of independent birth centers and home delivery believe that distance from the hospital is necessary to help avoid rigid protocols and standards of care that too often needlessly encourage medical interventions. Recent research in the United States indicates a rise in the number of women choosing midwifery care at birth centers as well as at home, though the rate of increase is not nearly as pronounced as it is in other high-income nations (Martin et al. 2009).

One reason for the slower increase in births occurring in private homes or independent birth centers relative to Western Europe may be the outspoken anti–homebirth and anti–independent birth center stance of some maternal and infant health specialists. In October of 2006, the American College of Obstetrics and Gynecology (ACOG), the most powerful maternal and infant health organization in the world, published an official statement of policy on out-of-hospital births asserting that "the hospital, including a birthing center within the hospital complex ... is the safest setting for labor, delivery and the immediate postpartum" and that "ACOG strongly opposes out-of-hospital birth." The executive board's statement is based on the belief that although "labor and delivery is a physiological process that most women experience without complications, ... serious intrapartum complications may arise with little or no warning, even in low risk pregnancies."

From the American College of Obstetrics and Gynecology's perspective, birth is potentially dangerous and, therefore, should occur as close to medical facilities and technologies as possible. Some of the homebirth advocates who have participated in my research refer to this claim as the "just in case something bad happens" argument. This view is presumably shared by a majority of women in the United States, if the current obstetrician-attended hospital birth rate of 90 percent is any indication (Wagner, 2006). So, while home and birth-center deliveries and midwifery care are the norm for the majority of the world's population, midwives in the United States attend approximately 10 percent of deliveries in the hospital and only about 1 percent of deliveries at home. In the United States, choosing out-of-hospital birth, and especially homebirth, are at the conceptual edge of socially acceptable reproductive behavior. Prohibitions against home and birth-center delivery by the medical establishment[1] air in vivid media messages communicated through emergency birth programming such as the Discovery Health television series *Maternity Ward*. Several generations of socialization into childbirth as a medical event combine to make the decision to deliver at home attended by a midwife a relatively radical one in the United States.

Given the dominance of the medical model of birth, how do some women decide to bypass mainstream, obstetric care and to give birth at home attended by midwives? What are women asserting about the medical establishment and about their own bodies when they choose a home delivery with a midwife? Are they using homebirth as a form of social resistance? If so, what impact do their choices have on the health of their babies? How do midwives operate in a society where the vast majority of families and medical specialists deny their credibility as legitimate care providers? What can medical anthropologists do to help educate patients and health-care providers about the costs and benefits of specific birthing practices? And how can research and advocacy lead to social change? This book explores these questions.

In 2009, the National Center for Health Statistics published the most recent figures on maternal and infant health in the United States. This report indicates that the rate of cesarean section in the United States is now 31.8 percent, up from 5 percent in 1970, marking the 11th consecutive year of increase along with another record high (Martin et al., 2009). Researchers fault incentives within the health care system for the rise in cesareans, citing physicians' fears of malpractice lawsuits, higher reimbursement for surgical deliveries than for vaginal deliveries, and the lifestyle conveniences of having more "9–5 deliveries."

If the increase in surgical deliveries were associated with a decrease in maternal or infant mortality, researchers and maternal-child heath specialists might commend rising cesarean rates as an appropriate intervention and characterize this practice as evidence-based medicine. However, the United States has not reported a decrease in maternal mortality rates since 1982, and infant mortality rates that had been declining steadily since 1958 are now on the rise and have been since 2001. As the incidence of cesarean section rises, so do medical complications for mothers and babies, along with associated health care costs.

Cesareans can be lifesaving for mother and baby in rare circumstances, but as major abdominal surgeries, they carry several substantial risks. The health risks in later pregnancies include increased incidence of infertility, miscarriage, uterine ruptures, and bleeding complications. Perhaps of greatest concern is that cesarean sections result in maternal death three times more frequently than do normal vaginal deliveries (Declercq et al., 2007; MacDorman, Declercq, Menacker, & Malloy, 2006). Though increases in maternal mortality are partially explained

---

1. In this book, my participants and I use *medical establishment* to mean the group of acknowledged experts who control standards and practices in medicine.

by better reporting of deaths, maternal death rates rise as the number of unnecessary cesarean sections increases.

These surprising declines in indicators of infant and maternal well-being continue even though the United States currently spends significantly more per capita on primary health care than any other high-income nation, while simultaneously serving the lowest percentage of pregnant women. In the United States today, over 11 percent of non-Hispanic whites, 24 percent of African Americans, and 23 percent of Hispanic women are still unable to access prenatal care in the first trimester.[2] Together these numbers indicate that improvements in outcomes and access to care have not resulted from increases in expenditures or from the widespread application of standard, "high-tech" interventions in the birthplace.

Among high-income nations, the United States currently ranks 41st in maternal deaths and second to worst, or 32nd out of 33, for infant deaths. Several low-income nations, including Cuba and the Czech Republic, boast superior outcomes with significantly fewer dollars spent per capita. All of the nations where maternal and infant mortality rates are lower than the United States have two things in common—universal health care and midwives as the primary providers. These two solutions are linked because universal maternity care is made possible by the lower costs, reduced rates of unnecessary interventions, and improved health outcomes resulting from midwifery care that have been documented in more than 30 studies (e.g., de Jonge et al., 2009; Fullerton, Navarro, & Young, 2007; Janssen et al., 2009; Johnson & Daviss, 2005). The United States is the only high-income nation that has not embraced midwifery as a solution to rising costs and diminishing returns. With all of the evidence for the benefits of midwifery care, why do so many in the United States perceive midwifery care as substandard care? And how have we gotten to this point?

MIDWIFERY IN HISTORICAL AND CROSS-CULTURAL PERSPECTIVE

In early modern colonial America, as in Britain and elsewhere at that time, childbirth was predominantly a social occasion controlled by women. Births were semipublic events attended by small groups of female relatives, neighbors, and a midwife who assisted the mother and baby and bore witness to the birth for the purpose of later baptism. Historical sources are biased toward wealthy and middle-class women whose journals have survived, and so generalizations about the skills and practices of midwives are difficult to make. However, information on births throughout the eighteenth and nineteenth centuries suggests that difficult or obstructed births occurred in fewer than 5 percent of cases, and that midwives generally enjoyed remarkably good outcomes (Ulrich, 1990).

---

2. See the U.S. Senate's statement on health disparities at http://dpc.senate.gov/docs/fs-111-1-102.html or statehealthfacts.org for more information on maternal and infant health disparities by social race.

In the case of difficult deliveries, a barber-surgeon or physician could be called; however, until the mid-eighteenth century this action constituted a death knell for the child and perhaps for the mother. Thankfully, such horrible conclusions to a woman's labor were apparently quite rare. Several recent demographic studies have significantly revised previous assumptions about maternal mortality in childbirth, demonstrating that in the seventeenth and eighteenth centuries, the mother died in only about 1 percent of births (Hay, 2002). Whether the risk of occasional death in childbirth translated into pervasive fear and dread of the process is a matter of contention between historians. A majority of them (Crawford, 1990; Pollock, 1990) emphasize the traumatic potential of birth. According to Porter and Porter (1988) birth "terrorized a woman's heart" (p. 100). Others assert that because the usual outcome was a safe delivery, fear was likely not the predominant emotion associated with birth for most women (Hay, 2002). In fact, most women diarists in eighteenth-century America describe birth matter-of-factly with no overtones of fear or dread (Wertz & Wertz, 1989).

Historians who focus on pregnant women's supposed dread for their own well-being often ignore what must have been a very real source of anxiety—the risk of death or damage to the child. While precise, historical infant mortality rates are difficult to ascertain, all available evidence suggests that they were significantly higher than maternal mortality rates (Hay, 2002)—a pattern that is still the case today. Fear for the life of the unborn baby may have contributed to perceptions of risk in childbirth then as it does now, and this fear may have been an important factor in the gradual transition from female midwives to male surgeons or "man-midwives," as they were first called.

"Man-midwives" began to displace female midwives in the birthing chambers of upper-class British women in the early nineteenth century. Changes in American birth practices were often the direct result of new technologies and trends that occurred first in Britain and were later replicated in the United States. Historians point to two important developments—the invention and dissemination of the forceps by the Chamberlen family between 1620 and 1730 and the publication of several new medical texts reflecting a view of the female body as defective machine—as the beginning of the end for the second-oldest profession in the world. Midwives were systematically excluded from using forceps and forbidden from enrolling in formalized schools for doctors. Graduates of these schools later came to be known as "obstetricians"—a word that comes from the Latin root *obstare* and means "to stand opposite to" or "to obstruct."

Soon afterward, the development of medical texts with more accurate birthing anatomy significantly enhanced the understanding of the female body for those who could access them. This theoretical knowledge augmented the clinical observations made possible by the simultaneous growth of "lying-in" hospitals established for poor women during the eighteenth century. These changes signaled the final shift away from midwives as experts in childbirth toward formally educated, male physicians. The usurpation of the traditional midwife's role met with occasional but ineffectual protest related to the impropriety of men breeching the privacy of the birth room. Ultimately, the ascendance of male obstetricians succeeded in part due to the increasingly pejorative characterization of midwives through smear campaigns that painted them as backward and ignorant. Many of the midwives I interviewed stated that little has changed in the last 100 years and that this attitude still persists among some physicians today.

Historians also attribute the rise of male obstetricians to their ability to exaggerate risks involved in birth and then construct themselves as the ones best trained to deliver women from their fear (Luce & Pincus, 1998). Although most people in the nineteenth and early twentieth centuries believed birth was almost always a healthy, natural process, obstetricians actively campaigned to reverse prevailing public sentiment (Hay, 2002). They set out to make mothers fear the dangers of pregnancy and childbirth and to think of no precaution as excessive. The midwives I interviewed for this book offered the same explanations for the current political battles they face—doctors monopolizing technology and knowledge, making derogatory characterizations of midwives, and capitalizing on perceived fear and risk.

In the late nineteenth and early twentieth centuries, some doctors envisioned birthing care as an enterprise to be shared with trained midwives who could be responsible for the more tedious and mundane aspects of birth. Some historians fault American midwives for their own marginalization at this time, citing the refusal by many to participate in the increasingly popular training programs set up by male physicians (Wertz & Wertz, 1989). Regardless of where we place blame, the ultimate result was the displacement of midwives as the primary maternity care providers, though some continued to serve immigrants, the poor in urban areas, and women in difficult-to-reach rural communities in this capacity until the mid-twentieth century. By the early 1900s, the respect that midwives had held in the past had been largely destroyed—a casualty of the trend-setting choices made by the affluent women of eighteenth- and nineteenth-century British and American aristocracy.

The movement toward physician-attended birth was further solidified in the Victorian era (1837–1901) as male gynecologists and obstetricians gained even greater control and acceptance in the birthplace. The sentimental focus on female delicacy that characterized the "cult of domesticity" and "true womanhood" during this period emphasized the notion that civilized and refined women could not and should not tolerate the "degradation of childbirth" (Wertz & Wertz, 1989: 114). Enter the notion of childbirth without pain—a feat that was first achieved through the use of chloroform in labor in 1847. The converse of this logic was that "uncivilized" Mexican American and African American women did not suffer in childbirth to the extent that genteel white women did. An unintended result of this racist logic was the preservation of midwifery traditions among low-income, minority groups in the United States. Significant regional childbirth cultures including the Mexican American *parteras* of the southwest and the "granny midwives" of the African American south existed well into the late nineteenth and early twentieth centuries, while Euro-American midwives were completely displaced by physicians by the end of the Victorian era. Wealthy white women turned increasingly toward male obstetricians, while poor, rural, and minority women continued to deliver in their homes with midwives (Hay, 2002).

The exception to this rule was the lying-in hospital built to serve urban populations of poor, unmarried mothers and minority women. Training in these early maternity hospitals furthered the tendency to focus on birth as dangerous, traumatic, and prone to problems. Deaths and complications were high in early lying-in hospitals due to the unsanitary conditions that existed prior to the under-standing of germ theory and the lack of hand washing. These hospitals were the primary breeding grounds for deadly childbirth fever—a postpartum infection transmitted to women by nurses and physicians. Obstetricians trained in this envir-onment understandably came to see each birth as a potential disaster and every woman as a potential victim. These beliefs form the historical foundation for the contemporary medical management of childbirth in the United States.

A logical outgrowth of the perception of birth as dangerous and risky was its movement into the hospital—a move that did not prove safer for women and their babies. In 1900, only 5 percent of babies were born in the hospital. By 1935, 75 percent were born there, and in 1960, the trend reached 95 percent. Today, 99 percent of births in the United States take place in the hospital. Death rates did not decline during this period, as many assumed they should. Instead, they rose (Hay, 2002). In the 1920s, as middle-class women began having babies in the hospital in increasing numbers, the maternal mortality rate increased, rising from 60 deaths per 10,000 in 1915 to 63 per 10,000 in 1932. In urban areas where hospital births were more common, the maternal mortality rate was 74 per 10,000—substantially higher than the overall national rate. In addition, be-tween 1915 and 1929, infant deaths from birth injuries increased by more than 40 percent (Goer & Wheeler, 1999).

Though numerous factors are probably involved in changes in maternal and infant death rates over time, evidence shows that the movement into hospitals did not improve birthing outcomes. In all regions where data are available, this shift from home to hospital is associated with increased maternal and infant death and disease. The midwives I interviewed believe that as women agreed to move their births into the hospital, they took their final steps toward total dependence on a manmade obstetrical system. Homebirth midwives and mothers today are still struggling to carve out a small niche in this hospital birth monopoly.

CONTEMPORARY MIDWIVES
IN THE UNITED STATES

Two kinds of midwives are important for understanding the roots of the home-birth movement in the United States. The first, certified nurse midwives, are registered nurses who complete additional, educational requirements (usually at the master's-degree level) and clinical training specific to midwifery. They prac-tice legally in all 50 states, and they currently attend between 8 and 10 percent of all births in the United States. Certified nurse midwives practice almost exclu-sively in hospitals and birth centers, though 3 to 5 percent also attend the occa-sional home delivery when their malpractice insurance providers, hospital, and backup physicians do not strictly prohibit them. The certified nurse midwives who participated in my study felt that they had been forced to give up some freedoms like attending deliveries at home in exchange for benefits such as hospital privileges and a measure of acceptance from the medical establishment. These trade-offs are difficult for some because it leaves them in an in-between place where their power and autonomy as practitioners is tenuous. While they enjoy a greater measure of social acceptance than the second category of midwife I describe below, they are often still the first group of providers to go when hospitals face budget cuts.

A second category of midwives, called direct-entry midwives, consciously reject nursing school and enter directly into midwifery training through one or more of several educational routes that include formal accredited schools, distance-learning programs, apprenticeships with senior midwives, and internships at high-volume birth centers. Direct-entry midwives believe that birth is not a medical event, and most see nursing training as irrelevant to their practice at best and a potential method of medical indoctrination at worst. Direct-entry midwives work at home and in independent, freestanding birth centers not affiliated with hospitals, and they do not have hospital privileges. They occupy a highly marginalized position relative to the culturally sanctioned obstetrical hierarchy, attending between 1 and 2 percent of all births in the United States (Declercq, 2007; Wagner, 2006). Their legal statuses, training requirements, and processes for certification or licensure, where available, vary significantly by state. Direct-entry midwives do not practice under the supervision of a physician, nor do they typically have formalized, backup relationships with obstetricians who are willing to assist them with home-to-hospital transports and prenatal consultations. When direct-entry midwives transfer care because a formerly low-risk client is developing complications, they commonly transport to whomever is on call for "undoctored" patients—those who arrive at the hospital with no record of prenatal care.

The medical establishment sometimes refers to direct-entry midwives as "lay" midwives, though this term is outdated and considered insulting by many because it implies that the midwife has no training. Direct-entry midwives began the process of professionalization in the 1980s, and they now offer an international certification based on the North American Registry of Midwives' examination and a subsequent credentialing called the Certified Professional Midwife. However, even with this credentialing, they continue to occupy a marginalized space. In 26 states direct-entry midwifery is legal by licensure, certification, registration, or permit; and in the remaining 24 states, plus the District of Columbia, they are not legally protected. Penalties for illegal practice of midwifery range from misdemeanors to Class C felonies (Runes, 2004), and active legalization movements are underway in all states where direct-entry midwives are not legal providers. In two states, Oregon and Utah, direct-entry midwifery is legal, but state licensure is voluntary. Voluntary licensure means anyone can attend a delivery as a "traditional" midwife, but only state-licensed, direct-entry midwives can legally carry approved medications such as anti-hemorrhagic drugs and oxygen for neonatal resuscitation.

Direct-entry midwives' variable legal status, combined with their position outside the established obstetric care system, makes them an excellent example of what anthropologists call a "hidden population," or a group residing outside of easily accessible social institutions such as hospitals and clinics (Singer, Scott,

Wilson, Easton, & Weeks, 2001). Hidden populations are difficult to access for research and often remain unexamined and subject to superficial stereotypes. As a result, homebirths attended by direct-entry midwives remain a highly marginalized maternity care option in the United States even though, as mentioned above, several studies across a variety of cultural settings have demonstrated with remarkable consistency the safety, cost savings, and high client satisfaction rates associated with their care.

DIRECT-ENTRY MIDWIFE AND MEDICAL ANTHROPOLOGIST

In 1998, I moved to Eugene, Oregon, to begin work on a PhD in anthropology at the University of Oregon with a focus on the health effects of the transition from pastoralism to semi-nomadism and agriculture at an ancient archaeological site in the Middle East. I had just started my first class on the medical anthropology of living populations and was fascinated to find that the vast majority of the world's population still gives birth at home, surrounded by female relatives, friends, and a community midwife. As the class progressed, I was surprised to learn that birth outcomes in the United States are quite poor compared to those in the rest of the world, despite the fact that so much money and technology are thrown at the problem. Having a strong background in evolutionary biology, I began to question how our species could have survived and apparently thrived before birth became a medical/technological event in the twentieth century. Could human childbirth be so poorly adapted that almost one-third of all women require major surgery to give birth to a healthy infant? I was curious and wanted to know more.

One evening while mulling over this conundrum and searching for a brewery where I was supposed to meet fellow graduate students for beers, I found myself lost and in the parking lot of the Oregon School of Midwifery. After finding the pub (which turned out to be next door) and a few beers later, a plan for a research project with homebirth midwives in the United States began to take shape. To gain access to understudied homebirthers, I decided to enroll in a direct-entry midwifery-training program. I attended classes all day Mondays and Wednesdays at the midwifery school while completing my doctoral coursework on Tuesdays and Thursdays down the street at the University of Oregon. I fulfilled the requirements of my full-time graduate teaching fellowship by instructing several sections of "Introduction to Biological Anthropology" on Fridays, and I spent the weekends and evenings completing all of my homework, reading and preparing for examinations. In retrospect, I am not sure how I completed the next two-and-a-half years of my training, except that I was passionate about my new area of interest, and I rarely slept—which ended up being excellent practice for attending deliveries! I successfully completed my coursework for both degrees in two years and then spent six months writing and defending my dissertation research proposal, submitting grants, and identifying research sites where I could simultaneously apprentice for the "hands-on" clinical portion of my midwifery training and also collect information for my doctoral research.

I found the perfect apprenticeship in a practice run by four midwives in a Midwest college town.[3] I prepared to begin the applied stage of my midwifery training with the understanding that I would simultaneously collect data on the belief systems, practices, and health outcomes associated with homebirth and midwifery. Over the course of my research and apprenticeship, I assisted at more than 100 home deliveries, 15 home-to-hospital transports, more than 500 prenatal visits and hundreds of postpartum and well-baby exams. I also participated in the political organizing of the statewide midwifery association, professional peer reviews, and the breastfeeding support and playgroup meetings organized by the midwives' clients.

In addition to engaging in intensive participant-observation, I conducted interviews with 50 mothers, 20 midwives, and 10 obstetricians, and I analyzed clinical records for all births attended by midwives in the Midwest practice over a 15-year period. Other researchers have attempted to understand the world of homebirth through interviews with mothers and midwives; my study was the first to utilize direct observation in the form of participant-observation and mixed methods or what is called a "numbers and narratives" approach. My training as a midwife and medical anthropologist allowed me unprecedented access to the world of homebirth midwifery. Participating in homebirth care has helped me to identify the discontinuities between the real and ideal worlds of homebirth and, from an insider's perspective, to explore variations in the processes of homebirth.

After my apprenticeship in the Midwest, I went to work at a high-volume birth center on the Mexican border where babies are commonly born in the halls, the waiting room, and in cars because their mothers begin labor while waiting for hours in lines as they attempt to cross the bridge into the United States. At this birth center I once assisted in the delivery of a baby during a flash flood where I found myself wading hip-deep in water. The mother, who had clearly been through a lot in her life, simply muttered *"mucha agua"* (lots of water) as she delivered. I received my certification and license as a direct-entry midwife in Oregon in 2005 and continue to attend home deliveries in Corvallis, Oregon, and surrounding areas while working as a tenure-track professor at Oregon State University. My department is an applied one, and my colleagues, students, and university administrators have been supportive of my work as a midwife, acknowledging that my position as a biocultural medical anthologist and clinician provide me with a unique perspective. My research on the culture, biology, and political economy of homebirth continues here in Oregon, a state with some of the strongest laws honoring the practice of midwifery and a woman's right to choose a place of delivery and attendant. Unlike in the Midwestern state where I served as an apprentice, in Oregon I have the opportunity to study the ways homebirth midwifery care can

---

3. Because homebirth midwifery occupies a precarious legal position in this state and because midwives are commonly harassed, I have been careful to hide the precise location where I conducted this portion of my fieldwork.

be brought in from the margins and implemented as a public health solution for reaching underserved populations.

In the pages that follow, I attempt to provide an "experience near" (Singer et al., 2001) for those of you who have never seen a baby born into the hands of a midwife seated at the foot of a birth stool and surrounded by friends and family, while also discussing the key findings from my research. I integrate stories of mothers and midwives in hopes that an understanding of their complex motivations and experiences might allow us to move beyond superficial stereotypes of homebirthers as "irresponsible risk-takers," "religious fanatics," or "crazy liberals"—accusations that all of my study participants faced repeatedly as a result of their choice to deliver their babies at home with a midwife. I challenge you to suspend your assumptions about childbirth and to turn a critical lens inward on the practices and cultural norms that may feel "natural" or "right," holding open the possibility that they are primarily the result of socialization and cultural conditioning and not necessarily the only evidence-based option.

Chapter 2

Challenging Hospital Birth as Norm

Alternative Models of Childbearing

The American College of Obstetricians and Gynecologists (ACOG) reiterates its long-standing opposition to home births. While childbirth is a normal physiologic process that most women experience without problems, monitoring of both the woman and the fetus during labor and delivery in a hospital or accredited birthing center is essential because complications can arise with little or no warning even among women with low-risk pregnancies.

ACOG acknowledges a woman's right to make informed decisions regarding her delivery and to have a choice in choosing her health care provider, but ACOG does not support programs that advocate for, or individuals who provide, home births.... ACOG encourages all pregnant women to get prenatal care and to make a birth plan. The main goal should be a healthy and safe outcome for both mother and baby. Choosing to deliver a baby at home, however, is to place the process of giving birth over the goal of having a healthy baby.

—The American College of Obstetrics and Gynecology's Position Statement on Home Birth, 2008

The Midwives Model of Care is based on the fact that pregnancy and birth are normal processes. The Midwives Model of Care includes:

- Monitoring the physical, psychological, and social well-being of the mother through the childbearing cycle

- Providing the mother with individualized education, counseling, and prenatal care, continuous hands-on assistance during labor and delivery, and postpartum support

- Minimizing technological interventions

- Identifying and referring women who require obstetrical attention

The application of this woman-centered model has been proven to reduce the incidence of birth injury, trauma, and cesarean section.

—The Midwifery Task Force, Inc.[1]

DEFINING MEDICAL AND MIDWIFERY MODELS OF CARE

In 1982, sociologist Barbara Katz Rothman identified two diametrically opposed birthing paradigms that encompass the spectrum of possible beliefs about pregnancy and childbirth in the United States. She labeled these models the medical and midwifery models of care, pointing out that the former model—the model that informs the American College of Obstetrics and Gynecology's position statement cited above—characterizes pregnancy and birth as potentially dangerous, pathological, and in need of technological intervention and medical management by highly trained (mostly male) obstetricians. Under the medical model of care, women are passive objects upon which procedures such as vaginal exams and labor inductions are performed. Physicians, and not mothers, "deliver" babies under this model; women are "delivered" or "sectioned" by their doctors. Rothman was one of the first social scientists to question how a focus on the need for obstetricians and their tools affects birthing women's perceptions of themselves and their babies.

Rothman believed that the midwifery model of care, described in the second statement above, tends to see women as healthy and active participants in the birth process, as the experts on their own bodies and babies, and as the doers and givers of birth. The medical model, she asserted, has failed to arrive at a working model of women's bodies that does not take men as the comparative norm; it treats normal female reproductive processes as unusual, abnormal or diseased states. The midwifery model, in contrast, understands birth as a normal phase of life for most women. Pathological conditions affect some women, but pregnancy itself is not a disease state. As made explicit in the "The Midwives

---

1. In May of 1996, representatives of the Midwives Alliance of North America (MANA), the North American Registry of Midwives (NARM), the Midwifery Education Accreditation Council (MEAC), and Citizens for Midwifery (CfM) worked together to write a definition of what they called "The Midwives Model of Care." The goal was to create a consistent definition that all groups could use in communicating with health care decision makers. The Midwifery Task Force, a nonprofit organization, copyrights this definition.

Model of Care" statement, midwives believe that the vast majority of women proceed through pregnancy and birth without major complications, as long as they have access to healthy foods, adequate exercise, medical backup when necessary, and holistic, individualized, and supportive care.

A decade after Rothman first differentiated these models of care, medical anthropologist Robbie Davis-Floyd (1992) renamed and elaborated on birthing models. She provided a comprehensive listing of how "technocratic" and "holistic" models of care differ from each other (see Table 2.1). Davis-Floyd's ideas largely overlap with and encompass the distinctions initially proposed by Rothman, though she changed the label *medical* to *technocratic* to emphasize that the medical model of birth is a reflection of the larger cultural system in the United States that hyper-values technology. In this system, physicians who manage health and illness function as elite, technical experts (Davis-Floyd, 1992). Similarly, Davis-Floyd uses the term *holistic* instead of *midwifery* to emphasize that the midwifery model of birth is a reflection of a broader view of reality shared by

T A B L E   2.1   Comparison of Medical/Technocratic and Midwifery/ Holistic Models of Birth (modified from Davis-Floyd, 2004)

The Medical/Technocratic Model	The Midwifery/Holistic Model
woman = object	woman = subject
male body = norm	female body = norm
classifying, separating approach	holistic, integrating approach
mind is above, separate from body	mind and body are one
female body = defective machine	female body = healthy organism
pregnancy and birth inherently pathological	pregnancy and birth inherently healthy
doctor = technician	midwife = nurturer
hospital = factory	home = nurturing environment
baby = product	mother/baby inseparable unit
fetus separate from mother	baby and mother are one
fetus's safety pitted against mother's emotional needs	safety and emotional needs of mother and baby are same
best interests of mother and fetus antagonistic	good for mother = good for child
supremacy of technology	sufficiency of nature
importance of science, things	importance of people
action based on facts, measurements	action based on body knowledge and intuition
appropriate prenatal care is objective, scientific	best prenatal care stresses subjective, empathy, caring
baby's health during pregnancy ensured through drugs, tests, techniques	baby's health ensured by mother's physical and emotional health, attunement to baby

proponents of the holistic health movement who favor integrated clinical, social, and spiritual definitions of human health and illness.

Rothman and Davis-Floyd's work on childbirth models help to illustrate the extremes of beliefs about childbirth, ranging from the notion of the female body as defective machine in need of medical management under the technocratic paradigm to a view of the body as a healthy organism inherently capable of giving birth with watchful and compassionate support. Yet both researchers were careful to point out that few individuals, including obstetricians and midwives, adhere to one of these models exclusively: "Most lean more toward one or the other while espousing some elements of both" (Davis-Floyd, 1992, p. 158). Works by Rothman (1982), Davis-Floyd (1992, 2004), and others (e.g., Klassen, 2001) have been influential in helping medical anthropologists to develop conceptual frameworks that facilitate discussion about contrasting birth models. They also give us the tools and language to examine how the implementation of these models affects the health and well-being of mothers and babies.

However valuable as conceptual frameworks, models are not people, and they certainly do not predict how health care providers actually behave and conduct their practice. They also tell us little about how these models or conceptual frameworks help or hinder women as they transition into their new roles as mothers. During my fieldwork, I kept in mind the distinctions between the medical and midwifery models of care I had studied in school, and as I interviewed physicians and midwives, I could usually identify their adherence to components of one or the other. However, as I began to attend deliveries and to watch how midwives and obstetricians performed birthing care, and the ways they spoke to and interacted with their clients, I began to see more complexity as well as differences between real and ideal behaviors, the theoretical and the lived. In examining how these models unfold and play out on the ground, I was able to identify multiple models of midwifery care. By helping practitioners and researchers to move beyond the dichotomous categories of medical vs. midwifery models of care, it may be possible (1) to identify common ground between models, and thus improve collaboration across the home/hospital divide; and (2) to gain new insights that help to explain how homebirth midwives achieve superior outcomes without the technological interventions so common in modern obstetrics.

FROM SPIRITUAL MIDWIVES TO "MEDWIVES": MULTIPLE MODELS OF MIDWIFERY CARE

Several months into my fieldwork and after having attended deliveries with six different midwives, I began to recognize substantial variability in the ways homebirth midwives view each other and espouse their convictions about what midwifery should entail. Laurel,[2] a Native American midwife who directed the school where I completed the coursework for my midwifery degree, sketched

---

2. All names are pseudonyms used to protect the identities of study participants.

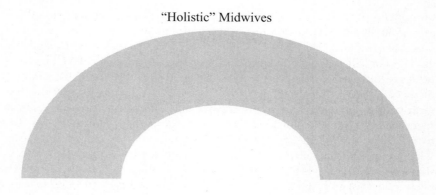

"Holistic" Midwives

Traditional Birth Attendants   Medicalized Midwives
"Radical"or "Spiritual"Midwives   "Medwives"

FIGURE 2.1 Continuum of midwifery models of care modified from a study participant's sketch.

a "continuum of midwifery models of care" during one of our interviews (see Figure 2.1). She explained that the space on the right of the spectrum represents certified nurse midwives (discussed in Chapter 1). Working primarily in hospitals with physicians, Laurel referred to these providers as *medwives*. The term *medwife* carries derogatory overtones; its use by many alternative care providers amounts to an insult and an accusation that a midwife is practicing according the medical or technocratic model of care. Most certified nurse midwives, Laurel asserted, rely heavily on technology and, though they may find ways to work around rigid hospital protocols, they often must surrender some of the ideals of midwifery for the security of practicing within the currently legitimized obstetric system.

Traditional birth attendants represent the opposite side of the spectrum. Laurel described traditional birth attendants as having little or no access to technology and a deep reliance on the wisdom of oral midwifery traditions passed down for generations. Although not regarded as acceptable providers for mothers in the United States, traditional birth attendants are often the only option for rural women in low-income nations. In the center of the continuum she placed "holistic midwives" and described them this way:

> In the middle, you have the majority of homebirth midwives in the United States, because they have tradition and knowledge passed down through a long line of women teaching women, but they also use technology when it serves the best interests of their clients. Care providers all along here [tracing the continuum with her finger] call themselves midwives, but they do not see birth the same way, and they surely do not practice it the same way.

The midwives I interviewed used different names to refer to and to distinguish between different types of midwives, and they were in general agreement that important differences do exist. Often midwives hold strong convictions about whose model of birthing care is most appropriate. What is acceptable practice for one group of midwives might be a criterion for demeaning a midwife in another group. For example, midwives embracing more technological approaches tended to have condescending attitudes toward a minority group of "church," "spiritual," or "religious" midwives who feel called by God to attend births for the women in their communities. The latter most often have no formal training and do not carry drugs for controlling maternal hemorrhages or neonatal resuscitation equipment to assist breathing in a struggling newborn. They "attend births on faith and herbs," as Lucinda put it. Their focus is on prayer and faith. One more medically trained homebirth midwife cynically said of "church" midwives: "Oh, let's pray, let's just pray over her and give her an herb while she bleeds when we could give her a shot of pitocin[3] and stop it [the hemorrhage] in two minutes."

Homebirth midwives who do not use any medications sometimes describe those who do as "medwives" or "interventionists." Such purists who self-identified as "less medical" or "nonmedical" believed that homebirth "medwives" did not have enough faith in birth as a natural process or that they had "bought into patriarchal messages of fear," especially if they were perceived as too quick to use medical interventions. To that accusation Lucinda, a self-professed "medwife," said, "Birth is natural, but so is death. Some midwives might think the most important thing is a hands-off homebirth, but really it's a healthy mother and baby!" Miriam, who self-identified as a shaman but was called a "medwife" by nonmedical midwives in her community, added, "They ['church' midwives] might be able to do 80 births and they won't need those skills, but sooner or later, if you practice long enough, you will need to do more than pray to save a baby or to help a mother."

Lucinda also believes that nonmedical midwives contribute to the current marginalization of home and birth-center deliveries in the United States:

> We cannot afford any guerilla midwives! They make us all look bad. The medical establishment thinks we are all like these "flaky let's just pray and maybe it will fix itself midwives." I know they are a tiny minority, but they get all the attention in the media. The majority of us realize we live in the twenty-first century and women and babies don't have to die or get sick from complications that killed mothers and babies 200 years ago.

As these quotes indicate, debates are sometimes quite heated among midwives who staunchly defend their version of the midwifery model of care. However, most midwives are open, at least in theory, to different ways of practicing and viewing birth. Several participants called my attention to the popular bumper sticker that reads "A midwife for every mother!" and the inclusive idea that it represents—the diversity of midwives should mirror the differing perspectives of women seeking homebirth care. These practitioners preach sisterhood and view mutual support among midwives as essential to the success of the political movements pushing to increase access to homebirth care that are active

---

3. Pitocin is a synthetic form of oxytocin, the hormone that causes uterine contractions. Pitocin is used in the hospital to speed up or induce labor and to stop postpartum hemorrhages. Pitocin is used in home deliveries only for hemorrhage.

all across the United States. Whether midwives engage in name calling—"guerilla," "radical," "church," "spiritual," "religious," "interventionist," "medwives"—or encourage sisterhood in the face of difference, their often-heated debates indicate that a wide variety of perspectives exist among homebirth midwives. Discussions during interviews, the debates that often arise at professional conferences, and, perhaps most importantly, the opportunity to listen to how midwives explain themselves to clients in consultations and prenatal visits provided me with a window into this diversity.

In reading over my field notes and midwives' interview texts, I was struck by several common themes and ideas that influence the expression of midwives' preferred models of care. I was able to identify five factors—(1) the midwife's level of experience, (2) the risk category of particular mothers and "rules for breaking rules," (3) barriers to practice, (4) physician backup and issues of legality, and (5) the midwife's own birth experiences—that strongly influence where midwives position themselves along the continuum of care. Perhaps most interestingly, these positions are not static. In observing hundreds of deliveries involving more than 30 different midwives, I discovered that midwives modify their views of birth over time and in response to the specific needs of individual clients. Midwives move with enormous fluidity along the spectrum of midwifery models of care in response to the collaborative dynamics of the mother-midwife care relationship.

"Birth Itself Teaches You": Education and Experience Level of Midwives

The midwives I worked with and interviewed were at various stages in their careers. Being able to attend deliveries with novice "baby midwives" and experienced "senior" or "grand" midwives provided insights into the ways education level and experience influence birthing care. Experience levels ranged from a student midwife who had just completed school and had observed only five births to an older midwife who had been practicing for 40 years and had attended more than 1,700 home deliveries. In addition, because I had undergone the transition from student to licensed and certified midwife myself over the course of this research, I could reflect back on my field notes and see how my own model of birthing care changed as I gained more experience and education on the job.

Several of the older midwives who participated in this study emphasized the extent to which "birth itself teaches you" and how, over time, experience alters views and approaches to care. The most experienced midwives, i.e., "grand midwives" (those with more than 15 years of experience and 500+ deliveries), reflected on their earlier days of practice and described how idealistic they had been. Lucinda explained:

> The first five years that you have anything to do with birth and midwifery, it is very easy to get caught up in the ideology of the entire thing. And then if you pay attention and attend enough women,

eventually something happens to reign in the idealism. That happened to me on the fourth birth I did myself as the primary midwife.... It was a really bad shoulder dystocia.[4] I thought homebirth was going to be all of these really sweet people, burning candles and chanting, and being intuitive. And instead I was faced with a real obstetric emergency. She was a good friend and her baby was very stuck.... But I handled it, got the baby out, resuscitated and everything was fine. I walked away from that thinking and wanting to learn as much as I could.

Lucinda believes that all or most midwives start out idealistic, defining themselves in complete opposition to the medical establishment as a way of defending their legitimacy as providers. However, as time passes and they do enough births to begin to experience the small percentage of deliveries that require technological intervention, their views shift. At this stage, midwives tend to move toward the middle of the spectrum, "picking and choosing the parts of the medical model that are helpful and serve the best interests of women" (Carmen) and rejecting the rest. Midwives in this study were in agreement that 90 percent of babies could be born at home without substantial intervention. As Miriam explained: "Ninety percent of the time, a monkey can catch a baby. The other 10 percent of the time you want someone with a bigger brain!" Experience with this small number of more difficult births, she asserted, instigated a shift from what she referred to as "the almost blind acceptance of the birth as natural model" to a more realistic and pragmatic approach—a model that had at its core the notion that "trust in the inherent safety of birth is usually, but not always, valued over technological intervention."

Change over time in response to experience level is also evident in my field-note journal. While I was a student midwife attending hospital births in Oregon, I was critical of highly invasive hospital procedures and the tendency to use pitocin for labor augmentation before first trying more subtle interventions such as getting a mother up to walk. My first few months in the field in the Midwest attending homebirths largely confirmed these perceptions because the first 18 deliveries I observed were relatively quick and straightforward. My early field-note entries are characterized by a focus on how few interventions occur during homebirths.

> I asked Lucinda today about all the spaces to record complications on the chart. There are spaces for time when pushing starts, head seen, crowning, head delivered, baby born, placenta, etc. and pages and pages for recording fetal heart tones. In all of the births I've seen so far, the mom gets on the birth stool, starts to push and the baby comes flying out. There is also so much equipment on the tray, and we never seem

---

4. A shoulder dystocia is a true obstetric emergency where the baby's shoulders become lodged behind the mother's pubic bone after the head delivers. Midwives and obstetricians are trained to intervene in this complication through a number of different techniques that are usually, but not always, successful. Shoulder dystocias are rare, occurring in fewer than one in 100 deliveries.

to use any of it. Lucinda just shook her head and said: "We'll talk about all of this after you've observed more deliveries." (Field notes, February 2001)

Now, hundreds of births later, those entries strike me as naive. I had not yet observed a complicated homebirth. A few months into my fieldwork, a woman's labor stalled for several hours at 7 centimeters, and the midwife transferred her to the hospital for an epidural,[5] pitocin augmentation, and a vaginal birth attended by the backup physician. In this case, all the midwives' "tricks of the trade" could not resolve the stalled labor or facilitate the birth at home. Lucinda explained that this was precisely why she thought the popular homebirth bumper sticker that reads "Every birth a homebirth!" should actually say "*Almost* every birth a homebirth!" The midwifery model of care I held during the classroom portion of my training was quite different from the model I hold now as a practicing midwife and researcher. Now I am closer to the middle or even more toward the right of middle on the continuum of homebirth care.

Individualized Risk Assessment and "Rules for Breaking Rules"

After attending more deliveries, I began to realize that midwives tend to adjust their models and practices to deal with mothers who have distinctive viewpoints or special needs. For example, in a few cases I observed some "hands-off" midwives ordering all kinds of diagnostic testing and even consulting with an obstetrician. This precaution occurred in the obvious instances where mothers were showing signs of a complication, but I also noticed that the midwife sometimes ordered testing when she had few or no concerns over the risk level of a client, explaining that her actions were "just to make the mother feel safe" (Carmen). The opposite was also true. Knowing that a woman was adamantly opposed to technological assessment and that she was at low risk for birth complications, a midwife might suspend normal tests and precautions to accommodate the beliefs of the client. The longer I worked with particular midwives, the harder it was for me to label them and locate their practice styles on the continuum of care. A couple of deliveries stand out in this respect.

One healthy, low-risk mother and her husband asserted that they did not want any ultrasound technology used during the prenatal period or at their delivery. Katie (the mother) believed that babies were "designed to be born and did not need to be monitored" using a technology that she felt had not been proven safe. She requested instead that we monitor fetal heart tones with an older technology called a "fetoscope" so that it would not expose the baby to

---

5. Epidural anesthesia involves the placement of a small tube or catheter into the epidural space surrounding the spinal cord. A combination of medications, usually a narcotic such as fentanyl or morphine and an anesthetic like bupivacaine, chloroprocaine, or lidocaine, are administered through continuous infusion. Together these medications block nerve impulses in the lower spinal segments, decreasing pain and other sensations in the lower half of the body. About 75 percent of women giving birth in the hospital in the United States do so with epidurals.

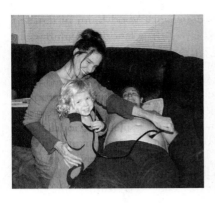

PHOTO 2.1   Fetoscope in use at a prenatal visit (photograph by Nicholas Saemenes)

ultrasound waves (see Photo 2.1). Carmen, the midwife, told me previously that she was opposed to mothers laboring without intermittent ultrasound heart monitoring, especially during the pushing phase of delivery, which was precisely the time when babies needed to be most closely and accurately monitored. Unfortunately, this is also the time when assessing heart tones with a fetoscope is most difficult because of the location of the fetal heart as the baby passes beneath the mother's pubic bone. Carmen affirmed this mother's faith in her body's ability to give birth unassisted by ultrasound technology, agreeing to use only a fetoscope unless she suspected a problem. The birth progressed without incident. During a later interview, Katie explained how this experience affirmed her faith in her body to give birth essentially unaided. Carmen demonstrated flexibility as she transitioned from her self-proclaimed identity as a "more medical than I used to be community midwife" to a "lower-tech" approach in order to meet the needs of this particular client. However, she made clear to me that she did so only because the mother was at such low risk for complications.

All of the midwives I interviewed emphasized that flexibility and individual assessment were central to the midwifery model of care regardless of their specific definition or version of it. Mary, another "grand" midwife, explained the need for flexibility in the following terms:

> Where a midwife sits on the continuum of care is actually highly moveable. I think that the best midwives sit in the middle and move in response to the needs of the particular client. If everything is moving along perfectly, you can remain very hands off and just focus on monitoring and providing support. But if things start to get off track, you can move to the other side of the spectrum and embrace more of the medical or interventive side of care to help bring things back in line with normal.

Even when women developed complications that made them moderate or higher risk, midwives were sometimes willing to "go out on a limb" if two criteria were met—what midwives called "true informed consent" and a relationship of trust. In the case of "true informed consent" midwives provide clients with information from both sides of a debate surrounding a specific care option and then determine that women have an adequate understanding of the ramifications associated with each choice and are able to make an informed decision. "True informed consent" differs from "supposed informed consent" where midwives or physicians promote their own agenda by providing partial or highly biased information. In "true informed consent," the practitioner must explain both sides of the argument as dispassionately as possible, encourage mothers to do further research, and allow them to make their own decisions. When this criterion was met, midwives occasionally bent their rules for clients whom they believed were offering "true informed consent" to either accept or decline an intervention.

In one case, Lucinda was facing a breech delivery (where the baby is presenting bottom- or feet-first) for a woman named Ellie who had had one previous cesarean delivery and a subsequent vaginal birth. This mother had read every article she could find in online medical journals; talked to doctors, midwives, and other mothers; weighed her previous experiences of a cesarean section and a successful vaginal birth; and arrived at the conclusion that she wanted a home delivery. Lucinda openly professes the belief that breeches should not be considered simple variations of normal, that they carry a higher risk than head-down or vertex presentations, and that breeches are best avoided by using a form of deep massage called "external version" to ensure that the baby delivers headfirst. She explained her position to Ellie, but she also told her that some midwives believe breech deliveries are a variation of normal, and that most obstetricians recommend a cesarean section for breech deliveries.

Because Ellie had heard both sides of the debate and engaged in thoughtful reflection, her case met the requirements for "true informed consent." Lucinda attended Ellie's breech birth at home because she believed that this mother fully understood the risk and was making an informed decision. On New Year's Eve, Ellie gave birth to her daughter, bottom first, gently and safely at home by candlelight. This is just one example of many instances of "rule breaking" I observed. All of the midwives I interviewed believe passionately in the use of "true informed consent" to help facilitate a woman's autonomy and right to choose.

The second criterion for rule breaking is a relationship of trust between mother and care provider as they enter an arena together that stretches the boundaries of what constitutes "appropriate midwifery care" and "low-risk delivery." Just where these boundaries lie differs substantially, even among homebirth midwives, and they continually shift based on the mother-midwife relationship. Although homebirth midwives do not all share the same boundaries in practice, all of the midwives who participated in this study shared stories about the times they were willing to cross or blur their personal boundaries under specific circumstances for special clients. A recent birth from my own practice stands out in this respect.

A few years ago, a close friend of mine, Cheri, hired me as her midwife. We grew even closer over the course of her prenatal care, establishing a relationship of deep trust and affection, and I was excited about the prospect of catching her baby. However, when Cheri went into labor, it was clear that her birth would not be easy. She labored at home for three days, making little progress. We ended up transporting her to the hospital where she labored for another 14 hours with the help of pitocin and an epidural. Then she pushed for three hours and brought the baby down to the point where we could see the head. The birth seemed imminent, but she could not deliver. We tried a vacuum extraction where a suction cup is attached to the baby's head and pulled as the mother pushes. Still no delivery. Cheri realized one of her worst fears—a cesarean section. When we brought the baby to her afterwards, Cheri said she did not believe it was hers. She had not felt her birth, and it "just didn't make sense" to her. I cared for Cheri through her postpartum experience as she struggled through a hospital-acquired infection, severe depression, and breastfeeding problems; we remained close friends.

One year later, Cheri confided in me that she did not bond with her baby until five months had passed and that when she got pregnant again, she needed to have a successful vaginal birth at home. She told me that Mozart's mother used to get him out of bed in the morning by playing all but the last note of one of his compositions. It drove him crazy, and he would inevitably come downstairs to play the last note. I realized that Cheri needed to play her last note. I felt her earnestness, knew she understood the risks, and although I did not think she was a good candidate for a home vaginal birth, I agreed to attend her. Against insurmountable odds and with several complications, she successfully delivered her second baby vaginally at home. Twenty-two months after her cesarean section, she got to play the last note. My attachment to Cheri and the opportunity I had to witness her struggle with surgical birth allowed me to break some of my rules on vaginal births after cesarean, to go out on a limb and to assist with a birth that would normally have been outside my boundaries. I am so glad I did.

Realities of "the Calling" and Barriers to Practice

All but one of the midwives who participated in my research discussed what they called the "honeymoon phase" of their midwifery careers. As they first learned about the homebirth renaissance, received their callings,[6] and became passionate about what many of them had thought of as a dead or dying art, they entered a phase of their careers where they were enamored with birthing mothers and the senior midwives they courted as teachers. They shared the joy and empowerment they experienced during those years of awakening with much excitement. However, they all eventually reached the pragmatic realization that extraordinary challenges faced them in sustaining practices in states where homebirth midwifery was either illegal or highly marginalized.

Homebirth midwives report struggles to maintain access to medications such as oxygen and pitocin, laboratory facilities, and physicians who are willing to

---

6. The midwives I interviewed shared "calling stories" that explained how they knew they wanted to become midwives. These stories often, though not always, have spiritual overtones and are marked as significant, life-changing events.

consult or provide diagnostic ultrasounds and other tests when necessary. In addition, because many are denied reimbursement from insurance companies, they face problems with clients who underpay, take a long time to pay, or are never able to pay. All of the midwives I interviewed had struggled financially for most of their careers; many had been on public assistance or lived in poverty for at least a portion of their training. Many had divorced or broken up with long-term partners in response to the stresses and the hardships associated with their calling. All of them mentioned the difficulty of keeping the long and irregular hours necessary to provide the personalized care associated with homebirth midwifery. The stresses of being on call with few if any breaks, the physical and emotional toll of attending long births, the financial hardships, and the political struggles all contribute to what midwives report is a relatively high burnout rate. Yet most continue to practice because of the joy that comes from being so close to what all described as "the miracle of birth" and the fulfilling experience of deepening relationships with families.

Lexi, a midwife and classmate during my training, described the early days of her practice as a "very expensive hobby." The midwives who participated in this study charged between $1,000 and $3,500 for their services. This fee includes all in-home prenatal care, labor and delivery, and six weeks of postpartum and well-baby care. The busiest midwives I interviewed attend approximately 50 births a year, though most reported 30 or fewer. Study participants gross between $10,000 and $40,000 per year and then invest some of that income back into equipment, upkeep, and transportation costs.

Midwives commonly attend women within a one-hour radius of where they live, traveling to their clients' homes for all or most of their care. The combined practice of four midwives where I apprenticed in the Midwest accepted clients in a two- to three-hour radius and traveled to their homes for the birth and all postpartum visits, as well as for most prenatal exams. During the year of my dissertation research, I put more than 35,000 miles on my car and once attended seven births in six days in five different cities trying to keep up with the demanding schedules of several midwives.

The busiest midwives have apprentices who can do some of the prenatal and postpartum visits or go out to check on a mother in early labor. However, the full responsibility for each family's care rests squarely on the shoulders of the primary midwife. Midwives, as a rule, are extraordinarily committed to what they call "continuity of care" and almost never miss a birth or a prenatal visit. Lucinda, for example, had attended more than 1,000 deliveries and could name the handful of births she had missed over the years due to illness, poor weather conditions, or another baby coming at the same time. Unlike in the hospital where shifts change and new nurses, midwives, and doctors rotate over the course of the labor and birth, the full range of care, with few exceptions, falls to a single midwife at home. After a long labor and birth, and no matter how tired, the midwife must clean up, complete the newborn examination, monitor the mother and baby for four to six hours, make sure nursing begins successfully, and then drive for up to two to three hours to return home, while at the same time remaining on call for other clients.

As a practice grows and the popularity of a particular midwife increases, the schedule of time-intensive care and sleeplessness also expands, inevitably requiring modification of the midwifery model of care. Midwives, for example, reported feeling pressured by competing obligations to arrive later in labor or to limit time spent at a prenatal visit. The demands on their personal lives also influence these tendencies to cut corners, especially for single mothers and those who are married and still have small children at home. Out of necessity, midwives sometimes feel pressured to compromise some of the ideal components of client care, such as lengthy discussions about emotional issues that typically arise in pregnancy. One midwife named Victoria explained: "It is hard to commit so much time and energy to the start of someone else's family when you know yours is suffering."

All of the midwives interviewed discussed the social and political changes that would have to occur to help reduce pressures and to make homebirth midwifery in the United States sustainable as it is in the Netherlands and the Scandinavian countries (DeVries, 2004; Harris, 2000; Walker, 2000). These changes include improving access to necessary medications, reliable medical reimbursement, more collaborative and amiable relationships with backup physicians, and the expansion of reproductive choice to include homebirth midwifery as a viable and more widely known option. A stronger infrastructure for the support of home delivery, midwives believe, will decrease the time they spend trying to work around the system, while also increasing the number of women requesting care who live within a reasonable driving radius.

The Dynamics of Physician Backup and Issues of Legality

Variations in midwifery models of care were further influenced by standards of care and legal statuses specific to each state and community. Some states prohibit direct-entry midwives—even those who are certified and/or licensed—from attending home births, though offenders are not actively pursued and prosecuted. In such states all midwives who practice outside the hospital setting are equally illegal and marginalized, regardless of whether they follow the protocols of certified nurse midwives (who are legal in all 50 states) or the protocols of "spiritual" or "church" midwives. Homebirth midwives who practice in states where they are outlawed have only personal ethics, fear of prosecution, and peer pressure to guide their views and practices of midwifery.

In Oregon, where I conducted part of my research, direct-entry midwifery has been legal for more than 30 years and licensed by the state since 1993. Licensed midwives in Oregon must adhere to explicit guidelines tied to their credentialing and oversight by the state. However, because obtaining a license is optional in Oregon, practicing as an unlicensed "traditional" midwife is perfectly legal, and the result is wide variation in how practitioners in this state perform their version of the midwifery model of care. The political, economic, and public health status of midwifery in Oregon has changed over the last 30 years due to the establishment of governing councils and licensing boards, leading to changes in the way midwives conduct their practice. Several experienced midwives discussed how their models of care changed as community standards of care shifted. Laurel explained:

> I tell prospective clients from the start that I used to be more radical, but I got older and more experienced and I became more accepting of some of what the medical model has to offer.... Things have changed so much since I began practicing. When we started out in the early '70s, hospitals were horrible, and they're not so horrible now. Back then, you didn't want to go to the hospital because they really did tie you up, shave you, give you an enema, and separate you from your baby and your family. Going in was seen as a last resort, and so we were more radical. We took more chances—pushed the envelope. They're no longer such horrible places and now my standard line is ... homebirth is not a place, it's a philosophy ... and it's about having healthy babies. We try things at home and the vast majority will go on to delivery with no or only minor interventions. But if we have to go in, at least in this community, we work with the doctors and we almost always get a beautiful and empowering vaginal birth in the hospital.

Laurel, like other grand midwives, asserted that her clientele had also changed over the last 30 years, as hospitals had improved in many places, making mothers more willing to go to the hospital and accept medical intervention earlier in a complicated labor. These nods of approval to the medical establishment aside, midwives still reject the predominant, technocratic model of birth in their respective communities. In fact, the most common theme in all of my interviews and informal conversations with midwives, both in legal and illegal states, was the passionate condemnation of hospital protocols, and especially of rising cesarean-section rates. Nonetheless, many midwives credit "largely superficial changes" in some hospitals, such as more homelike rooms and relaxed protocols on the number of guests allowed to be present for the birth, with making their clients less afraid of the hospital.

In states where homebirth midwifery is not legally protected, the midwives I interviewed had a different perspective on, and a more tenuous relationship with, the medical establishment, at least at the beginning of their careers. Lucinda recounted the story of a baby who died in the hospital several hours after arriving in an "appropriate transport" for early signs of fetal distress. She believed that hospital staff members were punishing the mother for attempting a homebirth. She and the mother "pleaded for a c-section for several hours before the baby died," while "they [the hospital caregivers] seemed determined to show us that we were overreacting and that nothing was wrong." From this experience, Lucinda learned to be careful about voicing her professional opinion—that is, never to trespass on physician territory by making a recommendation for treatment. She believes that many obstetricians are so opposed to homebirth midwives that "They are more invested in proving you don't know anything, than in working with you to treat an obvious complication." The difficulty of managing hospital transports and the frequent conflict between disparate midwifery and medical models of care were common themes in midwives' narratives. Over the course of my research, I observed several heated and bitter exchanges between obstetricians, nurses, and midwives, though I also observed them treating each other with mutual respect. I address problems with home-to-hospital transports in more detail in Chapter 6.

The availability of medical backup is particularly dire in some communities in the Midwest where authorities actively hunt and prosecute homebirth midwives. However, models of care, even in the Midwest, have changed over time, from more oppositional approaches to ones based on collaboration between medical personnel and midwives. For example, midwives in one illegal state solidified relationships with two obstetricians at a local hospital who felt it was a woman's right to choose where she would deliver her baby. In reflecting back on this important change, Miriam said,

> Those days of horrible transports are over—at least for now. We really have a highly effective setup here, even though we are not legal. Our backup doctor meets us at the hospital whenever we need additional assistance. It used to be that transports meant automatic c-sections for our clients, and so we were hesitant to go in. Now that we have someone who doesn't use surgical delivery as a punishment for women who attempt a homebirth, we almost always get an assisted vaginal birth.

Differences in medical backup arrangements, legal statuses, relationships with medical care providers, and governing boards in legal states influence the midwifery model of care advocated for and implemented by homebirth midwives.

Midwives' Own Birth Experiences

One phase of my research involved returning findings back to study participants so that they had the chance to critique or validate my interpretations. I also wanted to give them the opportunity to request changes in any details that might reveal their identity and jeopardize their practices. When I presented them with the results discussed in this chapter, all of them could think of instances when these factors—the midwife's level of experience, the risk category of particular mothers and "rules for breaking rules," barriers to practice, and physician backup and issues of legality—had influenced them and their midwifery colleagues. They expressed enormous support for my primary finding that there are multiple midwifery models of care and that the practice of midwifery changes over time and in relation to specific clients' needs.

Discussions of my results with midwives, however, revealed an additional factor that I had initially overlooked—the influence of the midwives' own birth experiences on their preferred models of care. Elizabeth, one of the midwives who critiqued my findings, asserted that the experience of delivering her own breech baby had deeply influenced her view of birth, and breech birth in particular. She views breech presentations as variations of normal, whereas some other midwives, as discussed previously, view a breech presentation as a complication best handled by technological interventions in the hospital.

In looking back over the transcripts of midwives' narratives obtained during interviews, I soon discovered that all of the midwives who had given birth to their own babies cited some example from their birth experience(s) that had influenced their model of midwifery care. Lucinda, for example, explained how the birth of her son affected her views of midwifery and medicine:

> Because of my own experience with Eric, I know that birth isn't always perfect. Because of my experience with my own child that died, I believe that birth is usually, but not always, a safe and fulfilling experience for a family.... Eric's birth was with an obstetrician in the hospital. I had every intervention possible, and he still died. That really influenced me and made me less likely to transport at the first sign of a minor complication or to put too much stock in the medical model. I don't rely on all that obstetrical mumbo jumbo to save the life of a baby. Technology can't always save the life of a baby. Sometimes technology actually hurts babies. And sometimes they just die. Occasionally technological interventions facilitate a birth that otherwise might not happen spontaneously. And so it's a compromise. Most of the time homebirth is just the most amazing, empowering and incredible thing. I love it so much. But you also need to know when technology can help ... though I recommend not putting blind faith in it. Finding the balance ... that's the art of midwifery.

All of the midwives who had given birth developed and adjusted their beliefs about birth and models of midwifery care in response to the memories, needs, challenges, and joys associated with their own birth experiences. Perhaps because I had not yet had my own baby, I simply overlooked this factor.

DEBUNKING "FAST FOOD" MODELS OF BIRTH

Midwifery models of care reflect the influences of numerous personal, political, legal, and clinical variables including, but not limited to, the five factors described above. Homebirth midwives move with enormous fluidity between embracing technology and adhering to "low-tech" or "hands-off" approaches as a means of addressing highly individualized client needs. The relatively rigid protocols (analogous to uniformly repetitive processes in producing fast food) observed by medical anthropologists in hospital births (Davis-Floyd & Davis, 1997; Davis-Floyd & St. John, 1998) contrast with the flexibility and collaboration between mother and midwife in home deliveries. A better understanding of the variation and fluidity inherent in the practice of midwifery may help to debunk the cultural myth that homebirth midwives are uniformly opposed to all medical interventions and have little or no formal training. My research suggests that although this may be true for the most radical extremes of some "church" or "spiritual" midwives, it does not accurately describe the vast majority of midwives currently practicing in the United States. In Chapter 6, I will show how the above misconception continues to fuel the ongoing oppression of homebirth midwives.

Second, my findings suggest that midwifery and medical models of care overlap today more than they did when Rothman (1982) and Davis-Floyd (1992) first articulated their respective birth models. This change is due, in part, to the professionalization of homebirth midwives but also to consumer demand for more humane and family-centered birthing environments in North American hospitals. I am hopeful that more widespread knowledge of this overlap, combined with greater physician awareness of the success of midwife-attended homebirth outcomes, will facilitate improved interactions across the medical/ midwifery model divide.

Finally, it is important to think about how the flexibility and individualized care associated with midwifery approaches may be influencing the safety statistics for home deliveries reported in Chapter 1. A more nuanced understanding of practitioners' birth models, and the latter's relationship to clinical and psychosocial outcomes, are important starting points in maternal-child health care research and reform. What are the mechanisms that contribute to the superior outcomes associated with midwifery care? Perhaps the effectiveness of midwifery can be explained, at least in part, by the implementation of flexible, time-intensive, and highly individualized models of care that are more closely aligned with the enormous biological variation inherent in human childbirth (Cheyney, 2005; Walrath, 2003, 2006; Zhang, Troendle, & Yancy, 2002). The kinds of variation in human deliveries that midwives allow to unfold without medical interventions include the length of labor (a few hours to several days), infant birth weights (five to twelve pounds), and weeks of gestation (35 to 43 weeks). Variation in the biology and duration of the birth process was discussed in detail by all of the homebirth midwives interviewed for this study. They described biological differences as "normal," "expected," and "much more varied than currently recognized by the dominant birthing paradigm."

Physicians also acknowledge variation in human birthing parameters, though the tendency in mainstream obstetrics has been to pathologize or deem "abnormal" cases that diverge "too far from the mean" (Walrath, 2003, 2006). The goal of many common obstetric interventions developed in the last 30 years has been to standardize the birth process and, thus, to decrease variation (Davis-Floyd & Cheyney, 2009). Induction and augmentation of labor with pitocin, for example, limit the length of gestation and the length of labor, respectively. Just how much variation is acceptable and what constitutes "too far" outside the norm is a matter of contention between medical doctors and midwives.

Medical approaches attribute variation in human birthing patterns to the "Three P's of Labor" (Cunningham et al., 2005). These "three Ps" refer to the **passageway** (the shape and size of the maternal pelvis), the **powers** (the strength of uterine contractions), and the **passenger** (the size and position of the baby in the maternal pelvis). Homebirth midwives add to these variables two additional Ps—the **psyche** (the mindset of the mother and the ways maternal emotions can either slow or facilitate birth) and the **position** (the position of the mother, whether she is upright and squatting to enlarge the pelvic opening or lying on her back in the "lithotomy" position, which inhibits the baby's rotation through the pelvis). Midwives claim that these five Ps combine differentially in women to create highly variable birthing dynamics, and that models of care must be similarly flexible and individualized to be effective. Under midwifery models of care, variation is normal for humans and not a problem to be fixed, altered, or decreased through technological interventions.

From this perspective, difficulties appear in the comparatively rigid guidelines used in hospital deliveries. For example, hospitals in the United States have long used Friedman's Curve for predicting and monitoring average lengths of labor, as well as for indicating when to require an intervention to speed delivery. In the latter instance, the standard according to Friedman's Curve is for the cervix to open at a rate of 1–2 cm per hour. Such standards are now subject to criticism even within the medical establishment. A recent study by Zhang, Troendle, and Yancy (2002), for example, examined lengths of unmedicated labors and challenged the validity of the widely used standard associated with Freidman's Curve. The authors show that the average time to reach "complete cervical dilation" (4 to 10 centimeters) during labor is actually closer to 5.5 hours and not the 2.5 hours previously thought to be the norm. Several other studies also recommend expanded definitions of the range of "normal" for the duration of maternal labor and fewer interventions to standardize its length according to an unrealistic model (Cesario, 2004; Diegmann, Andrews, & Niemczura, 2000).

Midwives in my study do not accept even the expanded definitions of "normal" recommended in the literature cited above. Instead, they advocate for individualized standards of care. As I discuss in more detail in Chapter 5, narrow, medical guidelines based on averages instead of on ranges, or other measures of variation, may be less appropriate for human mothers than the flexible and individualized definitions of what constitutes "normal" labor valued in most midwifery practices. As Mary explained, "Highly standardized 'fast food models' of birth just do not work very well for human mothers. You can use interventions like pitocin to force women onto the same page or you can acknowledge that different women birth differently and that what is not normal for one might be perfectly so for another.... The later approach simply produces better outcomes." The implementation of flexible birth models and the acceptance of a fairly wide range of "normal" under midwifery models of care is a result of homebirth midwives' personal observations. Attending numerous births in a time-intensive, individualized, and comprehensive manner provides insights often missed in hospital care, which is typically fragmented by the comings and goings of several providers who observe their patients for only a small portion of their overall prenatal care, labors, and deliveries.

SUMMARY AND CONCLUSION

From "spiritual" midwives to "medwives," multiple midwifery models of care exist today, more than 20 years after the development of Rothman's and Davis-Floyd's childbirth models. Interviews and participant-observation with midwives suggest that the midwifery model of care is itself best understood as a continuum of diverse views and approaches to childbirth. This continuum of care is multidimensional, dynamic, and flexible, and it varies according to several important factors, including the midwife's experience level, the risk category of particular mothers, and "rules for breaking rules," barriers to practice, physician backup and issues of legality, and the midwife's own birth experiences. In addition, I have proposed that the variation and flexibility within midwifery models of care may be better suited to the biocultural variability of unmedicated human birth. This compatibility between midwifery approaches and the biology of birth may partially explain the superior outcomes documented for homebirth midwifery in high-income nations. Homebirth midwives currently exist as a heavily suppressed minority in the United States where they are actively persecuted by law enforcement and explicitly opposed for their "subversive" views by the powerful medical establishment. Despite this suppression, midwifery models of care hold many clues for researchers and clinicians interested in improving the outcomes of birthing care.

Chapter 3

Performing Homebirth
Rituals of Transformation

Wе want mothers to reflect on their births, to be amazed at what they have done, and to fall madly in love with their babies. As women in this society, we are told that something is wrong with us at every turn. We have PMS that requires medications so we're not too moody. We need thousands of dollars worth of technology to get our babies out alive. Our breast milk is a burden, so we're offered a substitute. And then, finally, when all of our malfunctioning reproductive processes are over and our ovaries shrivel up, we can consider expensive hormone replacement therapy. The myth of the totally dysfunctional female body is big business! That's a lot to ask women to take in—to be made to feel totally incompetent. But then we're expected to perform the most difficult task there is, and that is to raise up new members of our society. Midwifery is about listening to all of that and then saying "I don't buy it!" If we can get women to trust their bodies and to trust birth, then that can lead to a total transformation for a woman. I have seen parenting from the position of victimization and from empowerment, and I am here to tell you they are not the same things. We're overturning unfounded notions about our bodies one birth at a time.

—Evie (homebirth mother and midwife)

In the early 1990s, symbolic and critical feminist anthropologist Robbie Davis-Floyd (of technocratic vs. holistic model fame) turned the lens of ritual analysis inward on hospital birth practices in the United States (1992). She pointed out that childbirth is not simply a medical event; it is also a heavily ritualized and socially important rite of passage. Davis-Floyd maintained that mainstream birth practices are designed to communicate the importance of technology as life saving and physicians as all-powerful in their roles as technical experts. Because child-birth is fundamentally centered on women, she believes that an examination of the ways a society treats and speaks about birth can reveal its foundational assumptions about the value of women as producers and reproducers. Almost 20 years later, most of Davis-Floyd's critiques of hospital birth practices in the United States as overly technological and unsupported by clinical research are still relevant. What has changed is the rising tide of outspoken dissent from mothers, midwives, advocates of natural birth, and a minority of physicians who are calling for the reform of a system they see as overly expensive, socially alien-ating, potentially dangerous, and unnecessarily dependent on interventionist technologies. In addition to making their voices heard, these critics are joining together to shape new practices and perspectives in opposition to dominant, obstetric approaches.

In this chapter, I examine the clinical practices of homebirth midwives in the United States and their clients from late pregnancy through the immediate post-partum period, evaluating them for their clinical efficacy (how effectively they produce the desired results) and for their symbolic content. I use Davis-Floyd's (1992) classic book, *Birth as an American Rite of Passage*, and her critique of tech-nocratic birthways as ritualized attempts to communicate society's deepest beliefs about the supremacy of technology as a comparative framework for examining the system-challenging practices of homebirth midwives. Using interview and participant-observation data collected from my years of fieldwork attending de-liveries both at home and in hospitals, I will show how midwives and mothers create and interpret meaning in childbirth, while intentionally employing ritual as a political tool for challenging the status quo of "high-tech" delivery. As mid-wives attempt to communicate the sufficiency of nature over the supremacy of technology, they replace mechanistic views of birth with the language of con-nection, celebration, power, transformation, and of mothers and babies as insep-arable units. Homebirth rituals actively challenge and, as we will see, in some cases, effectively reform the practices of technocratic birth.

A BRIEF HISTORY OF RESEARCH
ON RITUAL IN CHILDBIRTH

Davis-Floyd's (1992) interpretation of hospital birth in the United States as a heavily "medicalized" rite of passage relies on the work of early symbolic anthro-pologists such as Arnold van Gennep (1960) and Victor Turner (1969, 1974, 1977, 1979) who maintained that cross-culturally most major life transitions are inten-sively ritualized. Turner and van Gennep believed that people use ritual to help control the unknowns inherent in major life changes (for example, the transition from being a single person to being a married couple). By engaging in repetitive, standardized, and patterned—what anthropologists call "ritualized"—activities, people gain a sense of control over the unknown. Ritual provides comfort by helping people to know what to expect as they transition from a known social status to another, new, and unknown one. Because we grow up embedded in culture and exposed to rituals such as weddings, baby showers, and funerals all of our lives, many of the deeper messages communicated through rituals are hidden, remain invisible, or are normalized in a subconscious way even as we participate in them. It is only through the process of critical analysis, what ritual specialists call "de-familiarization," that we can begin to identify the veiled messages and values communicated through rites of passage.

During a rite of passage—defined as a series of rituals that move individuals from one status to another—participants exist in a transitional realm that is unlike either the previous status or the new status to come. Turner (1979) asserted that the out-of-the-ordinary nature of this realm facilitates a psychological opening or heightened awareness in participants (think of how you feel just before the bride walks down the aisle), and it communicates, reaffirms, and validates core beliefs (for example, the white dress as a symbol of the bride's purity). Childbirth contains the three stages of a rite of passage originally outlined by van Gennep (1960): (1) **separation** of the individual from her normal or previous social state (nonpregnant woman); (2) a period of **transition** where participants exist in a "liminal" or in-between space where they are not clearly one thing or another (pregnant and laboring mother-to-be); and (3) an **integration** phase where individuals are gradually reintegrated back into society replete with a new social state (mother of a new baby).

Childbirth is a time when mothers are open to guidance from others, and particularly from those considered "experts" on childbirth. By exploiting the inherently transformative properties of the birth process, a society can guarantee transmission of its basic values to participants. The ritualized practices characteristic of a typical hospital birth in the United States—the wheelchair, donning of the hospital gown, administration of intravenous (IV) fluids and medications, and electronic fetal monitoring—communicate the importance of technology in the birthplace and a birth-as-illness or birth-as-medical-event perspective. Based on hundreds of interviews with women who experienced hospital births, Davis-Floyd found that the final result of this rite of passage is a woman who "believes in science, relies on technology, recognizes her inferiority (either consciously or unconsciously)," and so at some level accepts the principles of birth as a medical event in need of massive technological intervention by the experts (Davis-Floyd, 1992, pp. 152–153). Such a woman is also likely to conform more broadly to the dictates of her culture, and thus, hospital birth is a profoundly effective way of socializing members of society from the inside, making them want to conform to social norms and values.

However, humans are not automatons, and the extent to which new mothers embrace the norms and values transmitted through hospital birthing rituals depends on the individual involved. Since in most cases the interventions of hospital caregivers are not absolutely essential to the birthing process, a window exists that women may slip through, avoiding the full extent of technocratic socialization. When birthing women sidestep obstetric standards of care, as when they refuse a procedure such as the placement of an IV line, they engage in what Butler (1997) calls the performance of "wrong norms." In doing so, they challenge the hegemony, or the rule by cultural consent, of medical models of care.

Davis-Floyd's interpretation of hospital birth procedures as ritualized practice derives from the semantic and semiotic schools of ritual analysis popular among anthropologists in the 1960s and later expanded by Turner (1969) and Geertz (1973) who viewed ritual as possessing characteristics analogous to language. Davis-Floyd's analysis illustrates this approach in its emphasis on the role of communication—the ideas, values, and attitudes that rituals transmit to participants. Performance-oriented approaches that emerged in the 1970s and continue to be prominent have a different focus as they examine how the symbolic activities employed in rituals enable participants to appropriate, modify, or reshape cultural values and ideals (Wirtz, 2007). Performance models focus on ritual actors as active, rather than passive, as makers of ritual and not simply receivers of messages. Ritual goes beyond molding participants, as participants often create rituals and use them to modify their worlds.

A third school of thought called "praxis approaches" focuses on ritual action as political practice (Nash, 2007; Paulson, 2006; Robins, 2006). Adherents see ritual as an activity that showcases cultural patterns and power relationships over time, and as a result, they tend to focus on processes of large-scale historical and social change. They view changes in ritual as indicators of changes in these processes. Because praxis approaches are particularly attentive to the political dimensions of ritual, they place emphasis on explaining how positions of domination and subordination are modified and resisted through ritual. In this chapter, I use an inclusive definition of ritual as symbolic message communicator, while invoking performance and political aspects of ritual in interpreting the clinical and ritual significance of homebirth midwifery practices. Performance and praxis approaches, when combined with classic, ritual-as-language approaches, illuminate homebirth practices as complex, dynamic, and intentionally manipulated rituals of resistance. In the pages that follow, we walk through pregnancy, labor, birth, and the early postpartum period together, exploring the deeper meanings of homebirth as ritual performance.

RITUALS OF TRANSFORMATION

Prenatal Care (the Separation Phase): Trust, Power, and the Rejection of Strange-Making

Pregnancy constitutes the separation phase of birth in a rite of passage; it begins with a woman's gradual partitioning from her former identity as nonpregnant woman and ends with her full acceptance and social recognition of her pregnant status. Medical approaches to the prenatal period focus on diagnostic testing and "fetal surveillance," the high-tech monitoring of the baby, and can function to extend the separation phase of birth as a rite of passage by producing a "tentative pregnancy" (Rothman, 1987a). As women wait to find out about the health of their fetuses, they may delay attachments and the acceptance of imminent motherhood, lingering in a tenuous, "wait and see" separation phase characterized by fears of possible complications. A participant named Anna said of her obstetric care, "I kept waiting for the bad news. Surely one of those tests would eventually show something was wrong. My doctor kept saying she might have to 'take the baby'—meaning do a c-section, I guess. When I went into labor a week early and had a nice, fast birth, I was actually surprised. I wish now that I could have trusted and just enjoyed my first pregnancy."

In addition, during the prenatal/separation phase, many physicians engage, though perhaps unwittingly, in "strange-making," the process of making the commonplace strange by juxtaposing it with the unfamiliar (Abrahams, 1973; Davis-Floyd, 2004). Complex medical terminologies label and sometimes connote negative judgments about the everyday, embodied experiences of pregnancy. For example, terms such as *false labor* and *irritable uterus* make relatively common pregnancy experiences seem out of the ordinary and can contribute to the sense of separation inherent in the prenatal period. Doctors also enhance the process of strange-making when they withhold (or perhaps do not having time to share) vital information about the birth process. By relying on alienating jargon, or "OB talk" as many mothers referred to it, doctors function as powerful ritual elders and elite knowledge-bearers who will necessarily take the responsibility for monitoring and eventually delivering the baby. Marshall, an obstetrician participant, embraced his position as ritual elder in saying, "I am all for women asking questions, but what they have to remember is that I have 20 years of experience and a frame of reference they can never have having one or two babies. I urge my patients to remember that I am the expert."

Mothers who experience mainstream obstetric care tend to internalize messages communicated during their prenatal visits to the doctor and can begin to perceive themselves as having little or nothing to add to the birthing process. As a result, they may complete their separation/pregnancy phase feeling vulnerable and beholden to their doctors or to the institution that will provide them with a healthy child (Davis-Floyd, 2004; Gamble & Creedy, 2009; Rothman, 1987b). As Eleanor bemoaned, "I am ashamed to admit it now after having a homebirth and really getting to live the difference between midwifery and obstetric approaches, but during my [obstetric] prenatal care with my first baby, I actually said to my sister that I wasn't going to contradict or question my doctor because he went to medical school and I didn't. I can't believe in retrospect how quick I was to discount the fact that I am the expert on my body and baby."

The homebirth midwives who participated in my research openly reject the messages of danger, uncertainty, fear, "tentative pregnancy," and doctor-as-ultimate-authority communicated by the rituals of mainstream prenatal care. Instead, they focus on encouraging the mother's connection with her baby and empowering her through knowledge sharing. During prenatal visits, midwives conduct the same diagnostic procedures as physicians, including urine screening, blood pressure and weight checks, fetal heart tone evaluation, palpation of the mother's belly for fetal positioning and growth assessment, and measurement of the uterus. These tasks take about 15 minutes and follow a ritualized pattern in that they occur in identical order at every prenatal visit.

However, in homebirth approaches, midwives teach women how to understand each procedure and attempt to make sure that "the flow of information is back and forth and not top down," as Carmen put it. They perform prenatal screening tests at every visit and describe them primarily as opportunities to foster reassurance, affirmation, and a sense of connection with the baby, and only secondarily as strategies for early detection and possible prevention of complications. They view knowledge as power and regard the bestowing of confidence and trust as central goals during the prenatal period. As a result, the vast majority of the one to one-and-one-half hours spent at each in-home prenatal visit involves "talking through" emotional and/or psychosocial concerns and either emphasizing the health and wellness of the pregnancy or discussing how to "get things back on track."

Through ritualized practices of pregnancy surveillance, combined with repetitive and intensive maternal reassurance, midwives affirm mothers as the ultimate authorities on their bodies and babies. In this process, they abandon notions about the supremacy of technology and build confidence in the sufficiency of nature. Eleanor said, "After just a few prenatal visits with my midwife, I started really feeling like I could do it—like other woman have birthed their babies, and so could I. I gained more and more confidence, and I rode that confidence like a wave through my birth into parenting." All of the mothers and midwives I interviewed recognized the need to monitor for potential complications, but none of them identified this as the primary reason for prenatal testing. Miriam explained that the key "is to affirm normality and empower women whenever possible, while also being diligent about risk assessment. The vast majority of pregnancies are normal after all. That is the art of midwifery—to be the safety patrol, but not to let talk of potential complications dominate the prenatal visits."

The obstetricians I observed and interviewed stated that they encourage prenatal monitoring primarily to help diagnose complications of pregnancy. They administer various tests at set intervals throughout the course of prenatal care, and patients rarely deviate from standard recommendations. Study participants who had experienced care with obstetricians and homebirth midwives (22 altogether) reported that visits to the doctor lasted between 15 and 20 minutes (usually after a one-hour wait) and that the visit ended immediately after the doctor completed standard prenatal procedures to rule out complications. None of these women felt that the doctors they saw met their needs for emotional support and help "working through fears," primarily because they saw several different and unfamiliar physicians in the practice over the course of their care.

Though some obstetricians may argue that affirmation, empowerment, and holistic well-being is either an inappropriate focus for prenatal care or that it should a take a backseat to more quantitative measures of maternal-fetal health, the doctors who participated in my study generally agreed that diet, exercise, and social support are the primary determinants of positive pregnancy outcomes. They simply were not able to offer psychosocial support or to employ preventative approaches due to time constraints and high patient volumes. In prioritizing their time, doctors choose (or feel forced to choose) to focus on screening for complications. Maria explained: "With the doctor, I felt like I was always waiting for something to go wrong. If everything was OK, that was more or less a fluke. It was the opposite with the midwives.... All through my midwifery care, I felt like I had a really great chance of everything being just fine. With my doctor I felt lucky to have gotten a living child!" Lisa added, "I hope no doctors or midwives are running around thinking all we want is a live baby and mother. How our prenatal care unfolds and how we feel about it does matter."

Ritualized midwifery practices that promote belief in the power and sufficiency of the birthing body, self-confidence, trust, and a sense of normality are strategies for overturning and avoiding the anxiety produced by strange-making and "OB talk." Midwives and physicians offer many of the same pregnancy surveillance procedures and often agree that the prenatal period is an extraordinary time when women are set apart from their former, nonpregnant status. However, midwifery and obstetric approaches to the prenatal period commonly differ in practice in their performance and message content. During homebirth midwifery care, the prenatal or separation phase is marked as special by honoring, celebrating, and reassuring the mother, rather than by imbuing the space with fear and tentativeness via strange-making, acceptance of the physician as expert, and (over)emphasizing testing for complications. Practices such as intensive client education and the shared interpretation of screening test results are rituals of empowerment used by midwives to influence the ways mothers see their birthing bodies. An enormous body of evidence documenting the benefits of holistic, socially supportive, and prevention-oriented approaches to prenatal care supports this approach (Hamilton & Lobel, 2008; Hazard, Callister, Birkhead, & Nichols, 2009; Hodnett, Gates, Hofmeyr, & Sakala, 2007; Zachariah, 2009).

Labor Care (Part I of the Transition Phase): "Mothering the Mother," "Fetal Monitoring" and "Keeping Things on Track"

From a ritual perspective, labor—the stage of the birthing process where the uterus contracts regularly and the cervix dilates—is a time of important symbolic and physiological opening. The stress, joy, anxiety, and pain associated with labor effectively facilitate the breakdown of everyday categories, often producing an altered reality and a "psychological opening" to the messages communicated through birth practices (Davis-Floyd, 1992, p. 39). During this period of openness, the symbols of a typical, medically managed labor, including the wheelchair, hospital gown, bracelet, IV, and electronic fetal monitor, dominate the birthing space and function to move the focus from mothers to machines (Davis-Floyd, 2004; Mitford, 1992; Oakley, 1984; Rothman, 1987b). As Elaine explained, "During my hospital birth, I was so over the focus on that damn monitor. Everyone kept staring at it saying, 'here comes another contraction,' and I was like, 'no shit!' Sometimes you wonder if anyone remembers there's a real, live person connected to the strip of paper they're so obsessed with."

In contrast, the purpose of homebirth midwifery care during this period is to initiate women into their new roles as mothers by modeling compassionate caregiving and supportive behaviors through what midwives call "mothering the mother." One-on-one, continuous physical and emotional support is a core principle of this approach. As a progressive labor pattern develops and uterine contractions become regular and challenging, the midwife provides non-pharmacological comfort measures including massage, heating pads, guided visualizations, and assistance with patterned breathing. Midwives, husbands, partners, and usually one or more family members or friends provide intensive, uninterrupted support for the woman throughout the entire length of her labor. Collectively they assist the mother and each other through each stage of labor and communicate to the mother that, though the main work of birthing is hers, she is not alone.

Both mothers and midwives assert that the challenges of labor contain many parallels to parenting. Birthing women, for example, often experience sleep deprivation, exhaustion, and concerns for the well-being of the baby during labor; these emotions or states of being will likely resurface many times as they parent a newborn. Through the intensity of their "pushed to the limit" experiences, mothers ideally learn to trust in their bodies and babies while acknowledging that they will need the support of others to meet the demands of birth and of early parenting.

Midwives use "birth mantras" or repetitive, formulaic sayings, spoken quietly to help soothe women through their contractions. These phrases include "don't fight it," "let your body do it," "open," "let it be strong," and "you're safe, just surrender." Aromatherapy, candlelight, and calming music are also common components of in-home labor care that capitalize on ritualized sensory manipulation to help women cope with the pain while simultaneously defining the laboring space as sacred, special, or out of the ordinary. Midwives consciously pull partners and other "birth guests" into the intimacy of the labor space by encouraging them to assist with comfort measures and verbal reassurance (see Photo 3.1). In this way they help to promote and solidify a support network for mothers that will extend through the postpartum period. Midwives believe that labor and birth participants will be transformed by the experience, and for family members and friends, this may translate into a deep and lasting commitment to the mother, her partner, and the new baby.

Homebirth midwives also have observed that upright positions speed labor, facilitate a mother's ability to provide self-comfort, and are safer for the baby; moreover, these observations are strongly supported by research (Downe, 2004; Lawrence Lewis, Hofmeyr, Dowswell, & Styles, 2009). In aiding upright posture and movement during labor, a midwife might ask "What feels best to you right now?" or give encouragement: "Listen to your body. You know what you need to do to birth this baby." Midwives also use various forms of hydrotherapy, especially birth tubs, to ease labor pains, referring to warm water emersion as "the midwife's epidural" (see Photo 3.2). Midwives encourage maternal vocalizations, termed "birth songs," as a way of coping with the intense energy of contractions. Their support strategies tend to be ritualized as midwives recommend patterned,

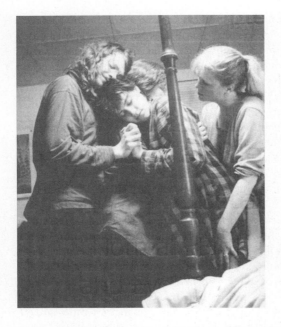

PHOTO 3.1
Continuous, hands-on labor support
provided by family, friends, and
midwives photograph by Claudio
Buchwald

PHOTO 3.2
Warm water submersion
used for pain manage-
ment and to encourage
upright laboring
photograph by Shayna
Rowher

repetitive position changes, vocalizations, and movement in and out of the water.
Through establishing routines of active self-comfort, mothers report feeling as if
they are "doing something, rather than just lying there passively waiting for contractions to happen" (Elaine), and this feeling contributes to a sense of personal
power and confidence.

Midwives monitor the physical well-being of mother and fetus throughout
the labor. They evaluate fetal heart tones every 30 minutes in active labor and
then every 15 minutes during transition—the most intense part of labor just before the pushing stage commences. They do this monitoring for the purposes of
making charts ("charting") but also as a way of reassuring mothers that they and

PHOTO 3.3

Midwife using a doppler to monitor heart tones photograph by Julie James

their babies are safe. Midwives use portable, handheld ultrasound devices called Dopplers to listen to fetal heart tones (see Photo 3.3). Because Dopplers do not require the mother to sit or lie in any particular position (as continuous, electronic fetal monitors do), women can remain spontaneously mobile and active during labor. Miriam summed up her role in labor this way: "I am there for comfort and for monitoring.... As the labor intensifies, some fear invariably creeps in. That's when I use heart tones to reassure a woman that her baby is OK. Yes, it's intense, but that is normal for birth. It doesn't mean anything is wrong. I am going to stay with her and help her. That kind of reassurance is really all most women need in labor."

Obstetricians who participated in this study were generally well aware that active, upright positions and continuous, emotional support speed labor. However, in hospitals women have difficulty in maintaining freedom of movement because of regulations such as continuous, electronic fetal monitoring and prophylactic, IV antibiotics given to all women who test positive for certain infections. When their movement is restricted during interventions or monitoring, women are more likely to request pain relief, which may further restrict movement, leading to a slowing of labor and the inability to push effectively (O'Connell, Hussain, Maclennan, & Lindow, 2003; Torvaldsen, Roberts, Bell, & Raynes-Greenow, 2004). This cascade of labor interventions is known as the "snowball effect" (Simpson & Atterbury, 2003; Tracy, Sullivan, Wang, Black, & Tracy, 2007). Many midwives and public health workers believe that this phenomenon is to blame for the dramatic increase in cesarean delivery rates over the last 25 years. As discussed in Chapter 1, the current rate of 31.8 percent is the highest ever recorded in U.S. history (Martin et al., 2009) and three times higher than that recommended by the World Health Organization (WHO, 2004).

Women who labor at home supported by their families and midwives, without the usual hospital interventions, receive powerful messages about their bodies and their abilities to birth. Homebirth mothers tend to emerge feeling that they and their immediate support network labored the child into the world, and not the institution or the obstetrician (Davis–Floyd, 2004). Whereas hospital births transmit the message that experts, institutions, and technologies produce babies, homebirth rituals communicate to women that they, in conjunction with their support networks, are the reproducers of babies.

Spontaneous, Upright Delivery (Part II of the Transition Phase): An Inversion of the Doctor-Up, Mother-Down Hierarchy

Once the cervix, or mouth of the uterus, is completely dilated and spontaneous pushing begins, midwives strongly encourage upright positions. I never heard a midwife tell a woman what position to assume to achieve the best results from pushing unless her progress was uncommonly slow, but many homebirth midwives provide birth stools and discuss the benefits of upright postures early in the prenatal period. Maternal positioning is usually on the birth stool, in the tub, or squatting, which typically requires that midwives situate themselves in front of and below the mother while sitting cross-legged on the floor (see Photo 3.4). Midwives organize their equipment around themselves for pragmatic ease of access but also gain psychological reassurance from utilizing the identical, "ritualized" equipment setup at each delivery.

Midwives encourage women to find their own rhythm as they push, offering continuous, enthusiastic support while often pushing along with them in what they call the "communal push." If a woman's strength lags during a particularly long or difficult pushing stage, midwives double their encouragements and offer her honey or other quick energy foods and fluids. If midwives judge progress to be unusually slow or stalled, they suggest maternal position changes. Once the baby descends past these "crux" (crucial) spots, the midwife encourages the mother to return to the position "she feels most effective in." Midwives assert that the ability to move around and change positions during the pushing stage, along with the use of upright postures that increase blood flow to the baby,

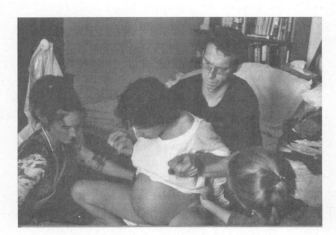

PHOTO 3.4

Mother-up/midwife-down positioning in home deliveries photograph by Julie James.

are vital for a safe and effective delivery. Again, substantial evidence supports their assertions (Bodner-Alder et al., 2003; Downe, 2004; Gupta & Hofmeyr, 2004). Most homebirth midwives diligently avoid the coached pushing used in hospitals. Miriam explained that the tendency in hospitals to have mothers push in a semi-sitting position in 10-count, coached intervals "makes pushing unnecessarily difficult … because it doesn't work with the mother's own natural, body rhythms and mechanics. Telling a woman when to push and for how long overrides her inner voice and the voices of all the woman who have come before her who intuitively knew how to give birth."

Midwives use many strategies to help women avoid trauma to the birth canal. Warm oil, hot compresses, and massage stimulate blood flow, keeping tissues supple, and flexion of the baby's head ensures that the smallest fetal cranial dimension presents during crowning. Midwives also encourage the mother to reach down and touch her infant's head as it begins to emerge. Along with verbal cues designed to help the mother to deliver slowly, touching the baby's head can sometimes help a woman to feel what she is doing and better moderate the speed of the final pushes. Midwives believe that collectively these techniques help to control the delivery, giving muscle and tissue time to stretch and avoid tearing. Fathers often help to "catch" the baby after the head has been assisted in delivery. Midwives refer to their role as "catching" babies unless the birth is difficult and requires manipulation to help free the infant. In these rare instances, their job is to "deliver" the baby.

Obstetrical viewpoints on pushing overlap with midwives' perspectives in some ways and differ significantly in others. All of the physicians I interviewed agreed that upright positions are the most beneficial for pushing and pointed to the inclusion of squatting bars on some contemporary hospital beds as evidence of this acknowledgment. However, doctors also reported that births in the squatting position are relatively infrequent in practice because of the high rate of epidural anesthesia. As Alan, an obstetrician, explained, "I'm sick of getting the blame for high rates of epidural use. It's not the physicians who are pushing them. Women come in begging for their epidural at 2 centimeters! How can they squat when they can't feel their legs?" Doctors also noted that the use of stirrups and pushing flat on one's back in the so-called lithotomy position have declined and instead, nurses or family members usually help to hold the mother's anesthetized legs back in a semi-reclined, knees-to-shoulders position. Although physicians acknowledge the clinical benefits of upright pushing, in practice, they rarely "deliver" babies in these positions.

With few exceptions, women experienced their pushing at home as empowering, active, and a welcome change from the contractions of labor. Most of the women I interviewed discussed the need to "find their own rhythm" as they pushed and how this required time and assistance from their midwives. All women who completed their births at home reported that when they were able to "follow the cues from their bodies," "work with urges," or "get the timing down," progress was clear and exciting. They enjoyed feeling the baby move down the birth canal even when they experienced this movement as painful. With the exception of the sensation of crowning, often called the "ring of fire," they recalled pushing with enormous joy and excitement. Bay described her pushing phase this way:

> I was on the birth stool, and as I got into the pushing, I could feel
> her coming down. It really burned and was intense, but I welcomed
> it because at that point I wanted to see her so badly. It was so hard.
> I pushed harder than I ever thought I could have ... but I loved it.
> I felt so strong, so unstoppable ... I can see why someone might want
> drugs—it does hurt—but I wouldn't want to be numbed for the good,
> no great, amazing feeling that comes with the hurt. I can still call on my
> experience when I need to and re-experience all that love and power.
> It was all so very, very worth it.

Unlike physicians' responses, midwives' and mothers' discussions of the pushing phase contain an interesting mixture of clinical and ritual significance. Upright, mother-led pushing not only increases blood flow to the infant, it also honors the woman's inherent intuition and body knowledge. In addition, the focus on upright, unmedicated pushing capitalizes on "symbolic inversion" where the gradual psychological opening to new messages characteristic of the liminal or transitional period of ritual is facilitated by metaphorically turning elements of the normal belief system upside-down or inside-out (Babcock, 1978).

In technocratic approaches to birthing, and especially where epidural rates are high, normal bodily patterns of interacting in the world are inverted as the woman finds herself with her legs widespread, her head lowered, preventing eye contact, and her vagina exposed to a room full of "intimate strangers." *Intimate strangers* is a term used by women to describe the nurses and doctors who participate in one of the most intimate experiences of their lives but are not well known to them (or known at all in many cases) before the onset of labor. In addition, women who are medicated may be unable to move or actively position themselves, contributing to sensations of vulnerability, powerlessness, and being "at the mercy" of her helpers during the pushing phase.

In contrast, the most common pushing positions at home are on a birth stool or squatting. The midwife's relative position, usually on the floor in front of and below her, produces a mother-up, midwife-down structure in opposition to the mother-down, doctor-up configuration characteristic of most hospital births. The symbolic ramifications of the mother's position on a birth stool are especially powerful. At the peak of this transformational experience surrounded by her family and care providers, Lisa described it as "feeling like a queen on my throne surrounded by my servants."

By encouraging mothers to do what feels best to them during pushing, and in offering coaching only if needed, midwives communicate the idea that mothers can tap into an intuitive, instinctive, body-level knowledge, and that "women's bodies know what to do to birth their babies." In contrast to the message that technology and the skills of the attendant avert potential disaster, midwives consciously attempt to communicate the power of the female body as a life-giving vessel. Midwives are careful to impart the notion that reflects their reality—that mothers deliver babies, fathers and midwives merely "catch" them.

The Immediate Postpartum Period (the Reintegration Phase):
Celebrating the Mother-Baby Unit

The early postpartum period marks the beginning of the reintegration phase of birth as a rite of passage where women are incorporated into their new social status as mothers. The rituals of the immediate postpartum period at home include the initial assessment of the baby, delivery of the placenta, delayed cord clamping, monitoring of maternal blood loss, and settling the new family into "the family bed" for the start of their "baby-moon." In the vast majority of homebirths, these are straightforward processes, as most mothers and babies who attempt delivery outside the hospital remain complication-free during and after the birth (Johnson & Daviss, 2005). Because pain medications and pitocin are not administered during labor at home, few infants require respiratory assistance, and most are vigorous and alert at birth.

At delivery, midwives make an initial assessment of the infant's well-being as they pass the baby up to the mother, placing the infant "skin-to-skin" (see Photo 3.5). They then dry and cover the baby with warm blankets and immediately conduct a closer examination of the baby in the mother's arms. As time passes they assign 1- and 5-minute Apgar scores.[1] One to two hours after delivery they conduct a thorough newborn examination at the mother's side (see

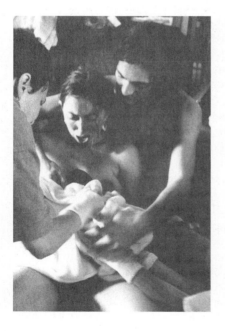

PHOTO 3.5

Baby being handed up to mother photograph by Julie James.

---

1. Apgar scores are the most common method of evaluating an infant's well-being; they are assigned in the hospital and at home at 1 and 5 minutes after delivery. A total score of 7–10 is considered to be normal, a score of 4–7 likely requires mild resuscitation of the infant, and a score of 3 or lower requires immediate attention to prevent a catastrophe.

PHOTO 3.6
Newborn examination
performed at the
mother's side as a way
of protecting
the mother-baby union
photograph by
Shayna Rowher.

Photo 3.6). Once mother and baby are assessed as stable, the father usually cuts the umbilical cord, but only after it has completely stopped pulsing and the placenta has delivered. This practice, called "delayed cord clamping," is an important component of how homebirth midwives see themselves as different from hospital practitioners. Midwives tend to feel strongly about how the immediate postpartum period should unfold and claim that it is cruel to separate mother and baby too early by cutting the cord just a few seconds after birth, as is currently done in most hospitals in the United States. Their feelings on this matter are an extension of the midwifery focus on early bonding, which they consider especially important when the infant requires assistance. Homebirth midwives assert that babies will be less stressed and therefore better able to breathe and regulate body temperature if their mothers remain in close contact, touching and talking to them, while their intact umbilical cords continue to pulse, delivering oxygen-rich blood.

All of the homebirth midwives I observed or interviewed were trained and certified in the same neonatal resuscitation procedures utilized in the hospital, and all carried portable oxygen and other resuscitation equipment considered essential for helping distressed babies to transition to extra-uterine life. However, midwives also advocate for some practices that differ from mainstream hospital resuscitation protocols. They maintain that resuscitation involves more than the physiological process of assisting respiration. They see infants as active participants in the process and, just as rescuers can coax adults back to consciousness after fainting by touching and speaking their names, so infants respond quickly to maternal touch and voice. Midwives, thus, encourage mothers to "call their babies back," to caress and speak to them as they undergo resuscitation.

"Calling the infant back" and delayed cord clamping have both been incorporated into homebirth midwives' regular Neonatal Resuscitation Program (NRP) trainings, and are well-supported by the clinical research (Emhamed, van Rheenen, & Brabin, 2004; Grajeda, Perez-Escamilla, & Dewey, 1997; Gupta & Ramji, 2002; Mercer, 2001; Mercer, McGrath, Hensman, Silver, & Oh, 2003; Rabe, Reynolds, & Diaz-Rossello, 2004; van Rheenen & Brabin, 2004), though none of the physician participants in my study were familiar with this literature.

Ken, an obstetrician, explained why they did not follow the latest clinical research: "Our standards of care come down to us from ACOG[2]—the supreme authority on how we are supposed to practice. It takes much more than new research to change a protocol once it has been established by ACOG." In this respect, midwives note that one of the few benefits of their marginalized status is the freedom to quickly change practices based on new clinical research. Physicians, who often find themselves entrenched in institutionally backed rituals, often have a more difficult time. Miriam explained:

> What we see right now is a lot of research coming out in support of what homebirth midwives have been doing for a long time like intermittent fetal monitoring and delayed cord clamping. We have known all of this because we trust birth ... and we have passed our knowledge down through many generations. The medical model has always thought they could improve on nature and little by little, as their technologies fail to significantly change outcomes, they are being forced to re-examine this. Unfortunately, because of deeply held beliefs in salvation through technology and women's bodies as pathological, plus all of the politics around for-profit medicine, this seems to be taking an excruciatingly long time!

Midwives assert that the ritual integration of the immediate postpartum period is not complete until the placenta or afterbirth delivers and the family has had a chance to celebrate the role played by this organ in "growing a healthy baby." Once mother and baby are cleaned up and nursing, birth guests gather around to observe as the midwife explains the basic anatomy of the placenta (see Photo 3.7). She holds up the amniotic sac or the "baby's house" for family members to see and encourages them to reflect on how the placenta nourished

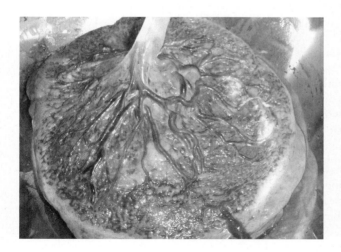

PHOTO 3.7

The "tree of life" on the fetal side of the placenta photograph by Jennifer Williams.

2. American College of Obstetrics and Gynecology (ACOG)

and protected the fetus during the previous nine months. Siblings often don gloves and help to examine and photograph the placenta.

All of the midwives interviewed and observed for this study discussed the deep respect they hold for placentas, "the most sophisticated life support organ on earth." The reasons for their reverence for the placenta include a highly scientific focus on its many functions, the fact that it is the only "disposable organ" grown in the human body, and its spiritual and metaphysical qualities. Metaphors for describing the power and mystery of the placenta include sibling, fetal home, and "tree of life." The tree of life metaphor was particularly common as midwives took care to show families the fetal side of the placenta and the pattern of vessels that resembles the branches of a tree. Some midwives also provide "placenta prints" for clients, made by pressing a fresh placenta against a sheet of watercolor paper to capture the unique vascular pattern. The placenta is not simply a biohazard or medical waste but is an important part of the birthing process and another opportunity for maternal affirmation and celebration. New mothers often store the placenta in the freezer for days or weeks until the final disposal, which most commonly involves ritualized burial or "returning the placenta to the earth."

Less commonly observed practices included eating the placenta after delivery in an attempt to mitigate the dramatic drop in maternal hormone levels that occurs in the first few days after birth. Some midwives believe a mother who consumes the placenta over the course of the early postpartum period, either in one of the placenta stews or other recipes circulated among homebirthers or in the form of dried placenta capsules, can help women avoid the "baby blues" as well as more severe postpartum depression. A few midwives also advocate, or are at least supportive of, a similarly uncommon placental ritual called "lotus birthing" where the umbilical cord remains intact for several days. The cord is never cut because mothers see severing of this maternal-infant tie as the first act of violence against the baby. In lotus births, the midwife wraps the placenta in a plastic-backed pad, covered with lavender, rosemary, sea salt, and other herbs, and the mother carries it around until the baby "releases" the cord.

The rituals of placental examination, celebration, and disposal communicate important messages to mothers about the sufficiency of their bodies and the sacredness or miraculous quality of their birth experiences. Midwives report that these foci, combined with feelings of elation related to endorphins, the natural opiates released during unmedicated deliveries, lead to a postpartum phenomenon many call "Superwoman Syndrome." In Superwoman Syndrome mothers feel so empowered and "high" immediately following the birth that they find it difficult to rest and take the time they need for recovery. Colleen explained:

> One problem we have is "Superwoman Syndrome" where moms think they can do anything after having an unmedicated vaginal birth at home. They feel great so quickly, especially compared to how they felt after their hospital birth with an epidural or maybe even a c-section. We want them to rest and allow their pelvic floor musculature to heal and strengthen, and there they are up calling everyone they know and trying to go back to doing it all.

"Superwoman Syndrome" is an example of somatization, where the personal power ritually communicated to and integrated by women as they claim their new identities as homebirthing mothers, literally becomes embedded in the body.

Davis-Floyd (2004) has documented the tendency for mothers giving birth in hospitals to recount delivery and early postpartum experiences as "battle narratives," or stories of harrowing triumph over "near death," complications, and unwanted interventions. In contrast, homebirthers in my study tended to recall the immediate postpartum period with joy and a sense of being in tune with their care providers. Their stories tended to downplay medical and technological interventions in retrospect, even for births that midwives discussed and charted as relatively complicated. This effect may be due in part to midwives' intentional glossing over clinical monitoring through their focus on the celebratory aspects of the birth. In doing so, they send the message that birth is as much a social and spiritual transformation as a physiological or clinical one. That women rarely mention postpartum monitoring or interventions suggests that this belief is effectively transmitted to homebirth participants.

Rituals of the immediate postpartum period at home also transmit the message that the mother's body is well-equipped to meet the needs of the newborn by providing oxygenated blood through the intact umbilical cord, comforting warmth during skin-to-skin contact, and nourishing colostrum, the first milk, from the breast. The supremacy of technology takes a backseat to the sufficiency of nature as midwives capitalize on the triumph, joy, and celebratory nature of the reintegration phase to enhance the maternal pride, power, and love they believe are essential components of healthy bonding and empowered mothering. Postpartum rituals also facilitate early bonding by keeping mother and baby close even during resuscitations, by encouraging "calling back" of the baby, and by providing the new family with privacy and carefully timed and unobtrusive monitoring. Davis-Floyd (2004) asserts that technocratic postpartum protocols send the messages that birth is a medical event, that mother and baby require close surveillance during dangerous extra-uterine transitions, and that technologies such as the isolette or warmer serve as symbols of the replacement of the mother's womb by the "womb" of culture. In contrast, homebirth midwives intentionally communicate the sufficiency of the mother's body and the celebratory over the clinical during the first few hours of newborn life.

FROM RITUAL TO RESISTANCE

Homebirth midwifery approaches are ritually elaborated clinical practices that can be transgressive insofar as they intentionally challenge and, in many cases, invert mainstream obstetrical messages. Midwives dispute the uncontested supremacy of science and technology, and the centrality of institutions and machines in the birthplace, as they focus on the holistic needs of women transitioning to motherhood. The obstetricians interviewed during my fieldwork claimed to be unaware of, though interested in learning about, the ritual significance of prenatal, labor, and postpartum care practices. According to their own reports, physicians spent little time reflecting on the meta-messages sent to women during childbirth. In contrast, the midwives who participated in this study have contemplated the symbolic meanings attached to medical models of birth at length and, as a result, actively construct alternative care rituals designed to eliminate disempowering messages about the female body, birth, and the mother-baby unit.

Women who internalize homebirth ideals in opposition to the core values of mainstream society may come to reject technocratic principles and instead embrace alternative perspectives on childbearing and childrearing. In performance approaches, "framing" refers to the process whereby alternative rituals facilitate the construction of new interpretive frameworks (Bell, 1997). These new frameworks, once established, become a tool to evaluate subsequent acts and messages. Women who successfully internalize views of their bodies as sufficient to meet the demands of labor and delivery also tend to "frame" their abilities to parent through such constructs. Thus, homebirth mothers are likely to embrace practices such as long-term, exclusive, on-demand breastfeeding; bed sharing; slings; cloth diapering; and attachment parenting. As a result of the same framing, they are likely to reject scheduled feedings and plastic baby-care devices such as bottles, cribs, swings, and strollers (Davis-Floyd & Cheyney, 2009).

The practices of homebirth midwifery care emphasize the holistic and celebratory nature of reproduction and childbirth as physical, social, and spiritual transformation. The fluidity with which homebirth midwives move between clinical diagnosis and psychosocial and spiritual interpretation communicates to their clients that the Cartesian mind-body split characteristic of biomedical paradigms (Davis-Floyd, 2001) is profoundly insufficient for explaining their experiences. The physiological processes of childbirth transport women into an inherently liminal space that carries its own affectivity. Homebirth midwifery practices capitalize on this affectivity to transmit transgressive values such as the rejection of the mind-body split and doctor as ultimate authority. From the perspective of homebirth as a subculture, this process is not successful unless the woman, child, and other birth participants are socialized into accepting the powerful and life-giving properties of the female body and the unity of mother and baby.

In addition to the symbolic content and clinical functions of homebirth practices, midwifery rituals are also self-consciously political in their intent. As the popular bumper sticker "Midwives: Changing the World One Birth at a Time" suggests, homebirth is a performance medium for the promotion of social change. Another popular bumper sticker reads "Peace on earth begins with birth. Support midwives!" Midwives and their clients assert that homebirth can lead to social transformation by empowering women to become grassroots activists, standing up against an obstetrical hierarchy that monopolizes the birthplace and removes women's choices about where and with whom to give birth (Boucher, Bennett, McFarlin, & Freeze, 2009; Craven, 2007). Thus, homebirth is a form of strategic ritual practice designed to restructure power relationships, and not simply a method for communicating messages about social norms.

In comparing hospital and homebirth care rituals I have identified real differences in the ways physicians and midwives think about and perform birthing care, as well as in the ways they communicate symbolic messages to their clients. In talking with participants and in observing hundreds of home and hospital deliveries, I cannot overstate the striking differences in the images, symbols, message content, and performances of these respective standards of care. However, midwives and doctors, at least in my study, differ more in practice than in theory. Pronounced dissimilarities in ritual performance appear to derive more from the institutionalized constraints of hospital protocols than from clinical evidence.

I was surprised to hear physicians discuss the benefits of many midwifery standards of care, including upright movement and position changes in labor, extensive one-on-one social support, lengthy prenatal visits that better address social and cultural determinants of health, pushing in the squatting position, and the benefits of close proximity between mother and baby in the immediate postpartum period. They express less agreement about delayed cord clamping and resuscitation in proximity to the mother; however, all of the physicians I interviewed claimed an interest in these practices. Physicians were unanimous in their observation that institutionalized restrictions put in place to protect hospitals and providers from litigation dictate the procedures they use as much or more than clinical research, and all felt powerless to substantially challenge or change these constraints.

The level of agreement between midwives and physicians about ideal birthing care in my study is particularly noteworthy given the growing body of research that documents discord between hospital-based practitioners and homebirth midwives (Cheyney & Everson, 2009; Davis-Floyd, 2003). Physicians may be supportive of midwifery care practices but still condemn homebirth as an unrealistic option, affirming the hospital as the only safe place for delivery. Similarly, midwives ceaselessly critique medical models of care, while simultaneously working to increase access to technologies, medications, and physicians as backup for their clients. The immense power of ritual to cloud, mask, or suspend logical thought may help to explain how professional caregivers are able to hold these seemingly contradictory beliefs. The existence of misunderstandings and conflict presents an important opportunity for medical anthropologists, who are trained to see the culture and power relationships behind so-called scientific medicine, to function as translators, helping physicians and midwives to speak across the ritually constructed and maintained home-hospital divide. I discuss this challenge in more detail in Chapter 6.

CONCLUSION: WHY CHILDBIRTH
RITUALS MATTER

In my research, I utilize a biocultural approach to medical anthropology that focuses on the interface of three factors that affect human health: (1) evolutionary biology; (2) cultural perceptions of illness and well-being; and (3) political-economy—or the ways differential access to power and wealth structure who gets sick and who stays healthy. The biocultural approach is an integrating perspective that attempts to bridge the gap between the biological and the social body. In this chapter, I have focused on childbirth practices in the United States as rituals that communicate messages to women about their bodies, their babies, and their places in society. And yet, from the perspective of biomedicine, it may not be obvious why birthing rituals matter, especially if the primary goal is a "healthy" mother and baby, where *healthy* is defined simply as the absence of disease.

Why are the ways we treat women in labor or the ways we socially construct childbirth important? The answers to these questions merge together what our society often thinks about as separate elements—physical health and emotional or psychological well-being. We have seen that birth rituals under midwifery models of care empower women and are important for a mother's psychosocial well-being, but do they actually affect the physical health of mothers and babies? Most cultures around the world do not acknowledge a separation between the mind and body and, as a result, assume that healing rituals and health interventions affect the whole person (Brown, 1998; Northrup, 2002). The complex connection between the mind and the body is an area that the health care system in the United States is only just beginning to recognize.

The study of the ways thoughts and emotions affect human health—the relatively new science of mind-body medicine—has moved from "heresy" to something approaching "wide acceptance" over the last 25 years. In its Integrative Neural Immune Program (a division of the National Institutes of Health), the United States government spent more than $16 million on mind-body research in 2006 alone,[3] marking an increase in the popularity and fundability of research that documents relationships between emotions and physiological states via the brain and its hormonal messengers. One mind-body area currently receiving research attention is the placebo effect, which refers to the recovery from, or improvement in, an illness in the absence of an active chemical or procedural intervention. Although the placebo effect has been widely recognized since the 1950s, researchers have only recently ceased to regard it as simply a feat of self-deception.

Recent studies indicate that placebo responses are not imaginary changes in symptoms, but physiological responses to measurable changes in brain chemistry (Brody, 2000; Evans, 2005; Johansen, Brox, & Flaten, 2003; Lichtigfield & Gillman, 2002; Roelofs et al., 2000; Sher, 2004). One often-cited study with Parkinson's disease sufferers, for example, demonstrated dramatic improvements in gait and grip strength in response to a mock surgery where physicians drilled a small hole into the patient's skull and then patched it over (McRae et al., 2004). The control group that received an already proven treatment experienced a significant rise in dopamine—a neurotransmitter that is lacking or reduced in Parkinson's sufferers. Surprisingly, the placebo group that received the sham surgery experienced the same increase in dopamine. Placebos are just one line of

---

3. See the Integrative Neural Immune Program's website at http://intramural.nimh.nih.gov/inip/.

research in mind-body science, and mounting evidence shows that any number of soothing emotional experiences including prayer, laughter, and meditation can improve physical health.

Long before the results from these and other studies began to filter into popular literature, midwives believed that women's mindsets or psyches played an important role in their birth outcomes. The intimacy of time-intensive and supportive prenatal care advocated by midwives, they assert, plays a decisive role in how a labor and delivery unfold. The calming presence of a midwife who develops an intimate relationship with a client over the course of her prenatal care is likely to lower levels of stress hormones such as cortisol and epinephrine that inhibit the effects of oxytocin—the hormone that stimulates labor contractions. The complex relationships between fear and pain and the hormones of labor may also help to explain "white coat" and "weekend" effects observed both in humans and in nonhuman primates (Jolly, 1999). These effects involve the lessening or complete cessation of labor contractions when birthing mothers know they are under observation by doctors or researchers.

The midwifery focus on "creating a climate of confidence," empowering mothers through intensive prenatal re-education, and the development of a relationship of trust between client and care provider contributes to a "less fearful mental space," as Miriam put it, through which women prepare themselves for labor and birth. Psychological effects may partially explain the positive results associated with homebirth care for low-risk women in high-income nations discussed in Chapter 1. Given what we know about hormonal messengers and their affects on maternal and infant biological states, rituals of mainstream technocratic birthing practices in the United States require further critical examination. Homebirth midwifery care strategies, in as far as they provide alternatives to the dominant medical model, are important starting points.

In conclusion, I have shown that homebirth midwives utilize alternative procedures and approaches to influence healthy birth outcomes, while also ritually elaborating evidence-based practices to capitalize on their symbolic potential to transmit messages about the birthing body. Homebirth participants perform alternative ideals of birth that stand in opposition to dominant technocratic models, while intentionally employing ritual as a political tool for creating a conceptual space where the "common sense" or "second nature" of the status quo may be questioned. Midwives and their clientele reject notions of their bodies as inferior or as necessarily in need of major medical intervention during the childbearing year. They redefine technology as a choice of last resort and regard it as ancillary to the innate wisdom and sufficiency of the unmedicated birthing body. They treat mother and baby as inseparable entities and reject the narrow, clinical focus of contemporary obstetrics in favor of celebratory and holistic notions of birth as a socially, physiologically, and spiritually transformative process. Birth at home, for them, is a ritualized act of resistance where participants actively create, live, and embody another way of giving birth.

Chapter 4

Narratives of Resistance
Homebirth as Biomedical Critique

On an extremely hot and humid afternoon in mid-July of 2001, I sat in the living room of a client's home for one of the many home visits I would participate in during my fieldwork. The midwives who trained me embraced a practice called the "home visit" where clients invited potential birth guests to attend the 37th-week prenatal visit. This allowed friends and family members the opportunity to meet the midwives, discuss the mother's birth plan, and have their fears and concerns about home delivery addressed before the onset of labor. I had by now participated in many of these visits and had come to call them "grandmother grillings" because of the tendency of the client's mother to passionately interrogate the midwives on the many real and imagined uncertainties of home delivery. "What if the baby doesn't breathe after delivery? What if my daughter hemorrhages or needs pain medications? Will you just sit by and take notes for your research while my daughter suffers?"

Lucinda always answered these questions calmly and with sincerity: "We carry oxygen and are certified in neonatal resuscitation. Hemorrhage, though uncommon, is a realistic possibility and so we carry the same medications that are administered in the hospital for hemorrhage. We give them through an injection in the thigh and, thankfully, they work very well to control bleeding. We are also very experienced and skilled at providing alternatives to drugs for pain relief like massage and warm water immersion in the birth tub or shower. Making sure your daughter has a safe and empowering birth are our first priorities." Lucinda, like so many other midwives, believes that if family members are left to themselves, their fears are likely to swell and eventually erupt during labor, often producing a dramatic scene that is the polar opposite of the peaceful calm most pregnant women envision for their home deliveries. During one of my first car rides to a home visit, Lucinda explained: "The most common procedure I perform as a midwife is a 'grandmotherectomy.' As labor gets really intense and it's hard for them to see their little girls in pain, their fears and concerns about delivering out of the hospital tend to flare up. I had one grandmother running around the living room hysterically screaming: 'Look what you're doing to her! You're making her suffer! Take her to the hospital and put her out of her misery!' She also threatened to call 911. After that, I decided to do my best to address family pressures and concerns before the birth."

Some of the women whose labors and deliveries I attended chose not to tell friends and family of their plans for homebirth until after the delivery. They believed that silence was the easiest way to avoid unwanted criticisms, dire predictions, and judgments on their sanity. However, the majority of study participants took advantage of their plans to give birth at home, using the opportunity to educate their communities on the safety and benefits of midwifery care. In doing so, they opened themselves up to enormous criticism from members of their social groups and from biomedical practitioners. During the early days of attending midwifery school in Oregon, I was struck by this theme as I listened to women's homebirth stories, and it led me to these questions: Given the pervasiveness of hospital delivery, the widespread cultural perception that homebirth is unsafe, and the institutionalized constraints that severely limit insurance reimbursement and access to physician backup when necessary, how do women arrive at the decision to give birth outside the hospital? How do they negotiate the fears associated with the "just in case something bad happens" argument that forms the foundation of hospital birth rationales?

To answer these questions, I drew inspiration from a subfield of medical anthropology called Critical Medical Anthropology. This school of thought was founded on the notion that health itself is profoundly political, and power relationships, like those that characterize obstetrics in the United States, are essential variables in health-related research, policy, and programming. The mission of Critical Medical Anthropology is expressly geared toward "emancipation"—meaning that its aim is not only to understand but also to change oppressive and exploitative patterns in the health care arena. Proponents of Critical Medical Anthropology see their work as essential because it can help to overturn the tendency for some domestic and international public health workers to affirm biomedicine as the only effective approach to health and healing (Greenwood, Lindebaum, Lock, & Young, 1988; Singer, 1990, 1995).

Adherents of Critical Medical Anthropology urge researchers to go beyond a focus on material improvements in health, such as increasing access to care for the poor, to identify and expose in their writings underlying power structures that serve oppressive ends. By unmasking sources of social inequity and by advocating for permanent changes in the alignment of social power, Critical Medical Anthropologists can have substantial and lasting impacts on the ways health care systems operate. Proponents of this approach are, by definition, applied anthropologists, as they seek to solve medical problems by altering the social and political contexts of disease through advocacy and policy reform—processes that are central to the goal of global health improvement.

As I contemplated the virtual monopoly American obstetrics holds over the rest of the world and alternative care providers such as midwives in the United States, the tenets of Critical Medical Anthropology seemed particularly appealing. In its explicit recognition of unequal power relationships, this approach offered an informative lens through which to understand and interpret the marginalized world of homebirth midwifery. As a biological anthropologist trained to collect information on measurable features of human biology, such as the length of active labor, birth weight, cervical dilation, and rates of various obstetric complications, I was acutely aware of the criticisms made by cultural anthropologists and feminist scholars (Cargo & Mercer, 2008; Higgins & Metzler, 2001; Israel, Schulz, Parker, & Becker, 2001) who point out that numbers alone are not always the best method for answering research questions. Purely quantitative approaches ultimately tell us little about the lived experiences of pregnancy, childbirth, and early parenting. Numbers may even obscure the faces and voices of those who live the experiences we describe with statistics.

Intimate and time-intensive ethnographic methods including participant-observation and serial, semistructured interviewing seemed well suited as I contemplated how best to understand the motivations and experiences behind women's birthing choices. The stories incorporated in the pages that follow illustrate the richness of these methods, allowing me remarkable access to women's experiences through the development of in-depth relationships between myself and study participants. Many of the women whose voices you will hear are still close friends who send photographs and email regularly to update me on how their home-born babies are growing into extraordinary children. Women's homebirth stories do indeed reveal motivations, personal struggles, and shifting sentiments that I might have missed if I had relied exclusively on numbers and "hard data."

COLLECTING HOMEBIRTH STORIES

I arrived at the tall university housing building a few minutes before the scheduled interview knowing it would take time to find the tiny cubicle where my study participants lived and worked as dorm supervisors. Jake and Julianna had given birth to their daughter Rose on their living-room floor a few months before, attended by two midwives and a knowledgeable and experienced doula. A doula is professional labor support person who specializes in hands-on comfort measures. This couple had enthusiastically volunteered for an interview as part of my research. When I arrived at the house, they welcomed me, served me tea, and took several photographs of me with Rose. As we transitioned to the interview and I took out my tape recorder, Jake handed me a set of audiotapes. "Uh, we got really excited and went ahead and already recorded our birth story. We also audio recorded the actual delivery, so that it is there for you too. Is that OK?" Jake and Julianna were doctoral candidates at a university in the Midwest town where I conducted the majority of my fieldwork. They explained that because others had given them so much support in their dissertation research, they were quite excited to help with mine. We sat together for the rest of the afternoon sharing birth photographs and discussing additional questions about how and why they chose a midwife for their delivery. Their participation in the interview was highly energetic and enthusiastic, their birth story punctuated with laughter and tears.

I had learned from my first interview during the pilot stage of my research that although childbirth may happen every minute of every day around the world, it is far from mundane for the women who experience it. Birth is often transformative and powerful, so much so that unmedicated childbirth frequently pushes women to the edge of what they feel they can withstand. Angela, a woman who told me the story of her home vaginal birth after having undergone a previous cesarean delivery, was overcome as she tried to put into words her experience of homebirth. She paused for a few moments and finally said, "I could never explain the power that passed through me that morning as I felt her moving down inside me, but I know it's the same power that makes the sun come up in the morning." Participants like Angela and Julianna wanted to share their birth stories and felt that the process of recording their experience gave credibility and value to a truly life-changing experience. I came to see that the sharing of their stories—the blood, sweat, pain, and, ultimately, the ecstasy of their deliveries—is central to how many women process and make sense of birth as a major life event that, as discussed in Chapter 3, ushers them from one social state (pregnant woman) to another (new mother). I sent 60 recruitment letters to homebirth clients, and remarkably all replied expressing the desire to be interviewed. Some like Julianna and Jake had already recorded their inter-views by the time I arrived. Others invited me back or called numerous times after the interview to add details to their stories. Willingness to participate was high even for women who had to be transported to the hospital during labor due to complications. Women wanted to share their homebirth experiences!

The answer to why women were so enthusiastic about sharing their stories even when they had less than ideal endings is related to my original research question about why women choose a home delivery. Women's stories reveal that homebirth is not just about selecting from one of several available forms of birthing care. The process of delivering at home is often a political act against an obstetric system that they see as wasteful and overly intrusive at best, and as traumatizing and disempowering to women and babies at worst. Furthermore, mothers' stories reveal that homebirth is not just a one-time act of resistance but a long-term process many described as "a journey" of redefining and re-claiming alternative forms of knowledge, of living the empowered body and rejecting what women often called "intimate strangers" in the birthplace. The very process of telling their stories to an interviewer who will analyze and write about them is a political act; it is a way of advocating for social change.

NARRATIVE ANALYSIS: INTERPRETING WOMEN'S STORIES

Anthropologists who study narratives distinguish between several categories of story that can provide us with windows into participants' experiences. Three of these categories—individual narratives, public narratives, and meta-narratives—are helpful for understanding the themes that emerged from women's homebirth stories. Individual narratives are highly personal accounts of our experiences that we develop through social interactions with other actors or participants in the story. **Individual narratives** help us to make sense of our experiences as we or-der events into cohesive chronicles that tell the listeners something about ourselves and the other players in the story. **Public narratives** differ from individual ones in that they are usually professionally or collectively produced. In the United States, for example, the medical establishment defines a set of recognizable public narratives around safe childbirth that usually involve hospital delivery with tech-nological intervention and obstetricians and nurses as attendants. Public narratives are more generalizable than individual narratives, and most members of a society are able to identify with the storyline. **Meta-narratives** are larger yet. They build on public narratives and carry the weight of culturally constructed expectations and deeply help traditions and values in which individuals and their social relations are embedded. Meta-narratives are so entrenched in cultural norms, the unspoken rules and guidelines that help to structure our social relationships and interactions, that the claims and assumptions underlying them may go unexamined; their implicit values seem "normal" or "natural" to us. The notion that childbirth is dangerous and requires medical intervention for reasons of safety is an example of a meta-narrative that exists in the United States. Guided by the above distinc-tions in narrative form, I identified three predominant themes in women's birth narratives: (1) redefining authoritative knowledge, (2) embodying personal power/ agency, and (3) creating connection/intimacy in the birthplace.

REDEFINING AUTHORITATIVE KNOWLEDGE

The first conceptual category, redefining authoritative knowledge, was the most com-mon theme shared in women's birthing narratives. Three associated sub-themes—unlearning and relearning, valuing embodied knowledge, and engaging in informed consent—help to explain the specific processes homebirthers participate in as they begin to challenge accepted public and meta-narratives of obstetrician-attended hospital delivery and reclaim an alternative body of knowledge.

Unlearning and Relearning a New Authoritative Knowledge

Women who shared their experiences with me constructed individual homebirth narratives, in part, as responses to what they saw as a limited set of culturally accepted public narratives on birthing options. In doing so, they were challenging what Brigitte Jordan ([1978] 1993, p. 152) has called "authoritative knowledge." Authoritative knowledge is the basis on which individuals make decisions and take actions, either because this knowledge explains the state of the world better (efficacy) or because it is associated with a stronger power base (structural superiority). In explaining why she chose to deliver her first baby at home even though her family "threatened to disown" her, Janine said:

> When I got pregnant, I was not going to be like all of my friends. You know the story.... They go overdue by a couple of days, go in for an induction that doesn't work, and they end up with a c-section. Then they're in too much pain and too depressed to nurse, so they have to find a support group to process their feelings of victimization. I didn't know much, but I knew I didn't want that. You're not supposed to say this in our society, but I'm not totally convinced that obstetricians really know what they're doing.

For Janine, the decision to give birth at home was embedded in a refutation of the cultural norm of the medical model of childbirth, a public narrative, and a challenge to obstetricians as indisputable experts and the exclusive holders of authoritative knowledge.

Homebirthers also dispute established hospital/public narratives to help resolve a lived discontinuity or disjunction between culturally defined birthing practices and their own experiences or those of close friends or family. Many medical anthropologists have discussed the difficulty of maintaining a sense of personhood and social identity through major life transitions such as childbirth. Under such conditions, the development of individual birthing narratives may facilitate the process of making sense out of what we sometimes call "biographical disruptions" (Bury, 1982), or the feelings of uncertainty and unpredictability that arise during a transformative experience like childbirth. However, periods of change also hold the potential for an overt clash and irreconcilability between individual experiences and cultural norms. Experiences with childbirth may produce a logical split between the "voice of medicine" (the technical details of birth as a medical event) and the "voice of the life world" (the social relationships and the experiences of the individual). Participants clearly articulated these discontinuities or splits in their efforts to give meaning and justification to their choice to deliver at home with a midwife. Kay explained this process as she compared her home and hospital deliveries:

> My hospital birth was horrible. My husband had to fire the doctor in the middle of pushing because he was insisting on giving me a

c-section.... It was so hard, because I knew that if I just had more time, I could do it.... We got a new doctor and I delivered vaginally after two hours of really difficult, but triumphant pushing.... With our second baby, there was no way we were going to subject ourselves to that kind of torment.... I wanted a midwife that I could trust, who believed in me and my ability to birth, and that is what we got with our homebirth.

Many women I interviewed described passing through a long and arduous process of "unlearning and relearning" as they sought a different kind of authoritative knowledge and "hungered for new information" and a "new way of seeing childbirth"—especially as they attempted to "make sense of what happened the first time" in previous hospital deliveries. They acquired alternative birthing knowledge through searching the Internet, reading books on midwife-attended births, and tapping into informal knowledge-sharing networks where women actively sought out midwives and other homebirthers who were willing to tell their stories. Elena, a first-time mother, explained:

When I got pregnant, I realized that I really knew very little about what to expect. So being an academic, I started reading everything I could get my hands on—books, Medline, mothering magazines. Knowledge acquisition was all I focused on for the first few months of pregnancy.... As I got more into the literature, it was really a process of unlearning and relearning. I had to replace all of those images from sitcoms where women are eating dinner in a restaurant and they suddenly go into labor and start screaming in pain while their husband runs around frantically.... Through reading, but also by talking to midwives and other homebirthers, I started to realize that as a healthy woman with a straightforward pregnancy, it was very likely that my birth would not be a terrifying emergency.

Despite "'what if' scare tactics" employed by the medical establishment, homebirth mothers overcame their fears of giving birth and justified their decision to deliver their babies with midwives outside of the hospital through their knowledge acquisition processes. One-on-one discussions with midwives were particularly important during this time. Amber said,

I had read all about the safety of midwives and homebirth, but I was still scared on some level. I couldn't really let all of my socialization go, and I was worried that something would go wrong. That lasted until I met my midwife. She was so confident and capable! Having seen all of those successful homebirths really put her in a different place, and she was able to put my fears at ease and help me know I could do it [birth at home].

All of the women I met during my research faced skepticism and accusations of "selfish irresponsibility" and "unnecessary risk-taking" from friends and family members who were not supportive of homebirth. Many of them noted that their own process of unlearning and relearning, though personally challenging, did not match the difficulty they faced in convincing their detractors. Cami lamented, "When I told my doctor I was thinking of having a homebirth, he said: 'Cool, and while you're at it, don't bother with a car seat!' … He totally discounted me even though I had printed out a full bibliography of over 100 studies on the safety of planned homebirth for low-risk mothers."

After experiencing a discontinuity between individual and public or meta-narratives of childbirth, homebirthers narrated a process of "moving" or "working through" a "journey" of unlearning and relearning that enabled them to start assembling new narratives that more closely modeled their own realities. These reformulated narratives commonly value new sources and definitions of knowledge. Participants discussed two in particular—embodied knowledge and informed consent.

Embodied Knowledge

The acquisition of formal and informal knowledge through books and storytelling were especially important during the prenatal period. However, in the context of labor, delivery, and the immediate postpartum phase, participants almost exclusively sought knowledge through intuition, that is, "embodied knowledge." They referred to multiple forms of, and terms for, concepts such as "instinct," "intuition," and "body knowledge" as a means of describing a way of knowing that was not intellectual, rational, or logical, but more bodily and experiential. Siri explained:

> My labor was taking forever and at one point I just started high stepping around the house … I was lifting my knees up to my chest with each step. I didn't really realize I was doing it at the time, but it just felt right and pretty soon after doing that I started to feel like I had to push.… Afterward, the midwives said it was really good that I had done that because the baby's head was tilted to one side, and by doing that, I was shifting my pelvis and encouraging the baby to move her head.… I just think it's really amazing that my body knew what to do. I wasn't conscious of it, but my body knew … I have a lot of respect for myself, for my body because of that. What if I had had an epidural? How could I have listened to my body?

Participants who discussed nonrational and embodied forms of knowledge also reported relying on childbirth education classes, books, the sharing of birth experiences with other women, and discussions with midwives as important sources of information. They valued both embodied and more rational forms of information as complementary and did not view nonrational ways of knowing as secondary or inferior to rational/logical forms of knowledge. As Lisa, a first-time mother, explained: "Education took much of the fear out of birth for me. But when it came down to it, I couldn't birth my baby with my brain. I had to go into my body and find what I needed to give birth."

Midwives also value intuition along with biomedical testing and measurable ways of rational or logical knowing. Occasionally, they even rely on intuition as a primary source of authoritative knowledge—a revolutionary act in a society that grants legal and conceptual legitimacy only to rational forms of knowing (Davis-Floyd, 2007). Midwives and homebirthers are laying claim to multiple, legitimate forms of authoritative knowledge. In doing so, they implicitly challenge the overreliance on technology and hyper-valuation of scientific ways of knowing that they believe reinforce the dominant paradigm of childbirth.

Informed Consent

In addition to embracing embodied knowledge, the women whose births I attended challenged public and meta-narratives of hospital delivery on the grounds that they felt a void of information and desired "better informed consent." Homebirth stories rely heavily on notions of information sharing and the co-construction of knowledge by midwife, mother, baby, and often the father or other family members. As discussed in Chapter 2, prenatal care with midwives entails discussing options for prenatal testing and interventions in substantial detail, encouraging mothers to ask questions and exploring the individualized pros and cons of procedures. This is how midwives believe "true informed consent" is achieved. In the more than 500 prenatal check-ups I observed, information sharing comprised the vast majority of the one to one-and-one-half hours spent at each visit. Midwives provide homebirth clientele with numerous handouts and encourage them to do their own research on common procedures such as ultrasound and amniocentesis. Homebirthers deeply value shared decision-making with their midwives and partners and, as a result, often feel empowered to make knowledgeable choices about whether to use specific technologies and interventions. Many participants agreed that "true informed choice is not possible in mainstream, hospital birthing care." Sarah, a mother who had a hospital delivery with her first child and a home delivery with her second child, stated,

> I really liked the co-decision-making process we had with the midwives. You know that you can't just surrender your body and say, "You make all of the decisions for me. You get this baby out." We were really involved in making choices about our care…. It makes sense that you get informed and make decisions about your pregnancy and birth because isn't that what you are going to have to do when you are a parent? The hospital might get a baby out for you, but they surely are not going to follow you home and help you raise it! Learning about birth was my practice for learning how to parent.

Alternative birthing knowledge that honors embodied and experiential ways of knowing and the co-construction of authoritative knowledge through informed consent allow women to create new realities and value systems around childbirth. They affirm these new realities through overt challenges to public and meta-narratives, as well as through direct action when they choose to birth at home as a means of avoiding a public narrative, that is, the medical model of birth. As families refuse participation in socially prescribed hospital birthing practices, they effectively undermine unequal power relationships between doctors as authorities and birthing woman as patients—an essential step in eliminating the inequality that obscures disparities in health care. In the major transition from dependence on external authorities (pubic and meta-narratives) to reliance on embodied knowledge or the "inner voice" (individual narratives), homebirth mothers often experience a sense of personal strength and power as they become their own authorities.

LIVING THE POWERFUL BODY

The acts of challenging a set of public and meta-narratives and of claiming a new authoritative knowledge are closely tied to a second key conceptual category incorporated in homebirth narratives—the acquisition of personal power and individual "agency," where agency is defined as the capacity to effect change and to make and carry out decisions. As women narrate the parts of their birthing stories that describe labor and delivery, passionate subplots emerge emphasizing the clash between public narratives and the lived experience of birth. Women's stories identify discontinuities, question the dominant paradigm of medical birth, and eventually claim an opposing story as real. These narratives contain three distinctive sub-themes related to personal power and agency: (1) knowledge as power; (2) empowerment as embedded in the intensity of labor and delivery; and (3) power as healing.

Knowledge as Power

All of the women interviewed discussed knowledge acquisition in connection with a sense of personal empowerment and the ability to affect their pregnancies and births through choice and direct action. Participants explicitly claimed knowledge as a form of power while asserting that withholding knowledge and limiting definitions of what counts as "legitimate" knowledge were disempowering. As Beth, a second-time mother, explained:

> In the hospital, the doctors and nurses are the experts and you are
> perceived to know very little, which actually might have been the
> case with my first baby (laughing). I felt like I never got very good
> explanations for why I was doing certain tests…. With the midwives,
> they spent most of their time with us sharing knowledge and asking
> me what I thought…. They said I was the expert on my body and my
> baby. I mean, can you see how that is a very different kind of message?
> Knowledge is power and in the hospital I didn't have the knowledge,
> so I didn't have the power.

In claiming the interconnections between knowledge and power, women are echoing the claims of a famous twentieth-century social philosopher, Michel Foucault (1982), who proposed that knowledge and power are actually synonymous terms. Foucault used "knowledge/power" as a single concept to express what he saw as the inseparable nature of knowledge and power. Because society through its representatives (governments, bureaucrats, educators, etc.) acknowledges the power of some groups (e.g., obstetricians) and limits that of others (e.g., midwives), the unexamined structure inherent in social relationships determines who holds the (legitimate) knowledge and therefore, the power. Disparities in power, Foucault asserts, lead to dominant and subjugated discourses, where "discourse" is defined as heavily politicized dialogues or debates. From the perspective of homebirth mothers, dominant and subjugated discourses are the medical and midwifery models of care, respectively. Through the acquisition of knowledge and the lived experience of personal power in birth, women who choose to deliver at home with midwives claim the subjugated discourse as real and, in doing so, reject the implicit claims of the dominant, public, and meta-narratives that favor hospital birth.

Foucault (1979, 1982) has also critiqued academic disciplines and the ways they induce submission to dominant discourses by promising rewards for compliance and punishments for noncompliance with their own social rules. With reference to the academic discipline of biomedicine, and childbirth in particular, hospital birth offers the rewards of safety, health, and pain relief for those who are compliant. When mothers reject the disciplinary power of obstetrics by birthing at home, society views them (and they view themselves, to some extent) as susceptible to the punishments of pain, death, and disability. Herein lies the power of social sanctioning—a mother who risks pain, death or disability, and harm to her infant certainly violates the social parameters of what constitutes a "good mother." Through the process of alternative knowledge acquisition, homebirthers challenge the assumption that contemporary obstetrics in the United States truly offers health and safety and reduces the likelihood of death and disability. Furthermore, participants do not regard the pain of childbirth as negative or something to be avoided. Ama, a mother who had had all three of her babies at home, explained:

> I of course grew up hearing the story that birth is inherently dangerous and unbearably painful and that I would need to go to the hospital to have a safe delivery. But after meeting a homebirth midwife and doing a lot of my own research when I was pregnant, I decided that that wasn't necessarily the case.... I also questioned the whole epidural thing.... We are taught that epidurals take away the pain, but really they take away all of the sensations including the power and the pleasure of birth. I wanted to feel my baby be born. Everyone thought I was crazy and irresponsible, but because I didn't see the pain of birth as a marker of danger or as something to be avoided, the hospital didn't have much to offer me.

Power as Embedded in the Intensity of Labor and Delivery

Homebirth narratives are interwoven with stories and subplots that communicate the enormous and often overwhelming personal power many experience as a result of the birthing process. A sense of exaltation and extraordinary accomplishment pervades all of the narratives, and several of the women I interviewed described the moment of delivery and the sensation of first touching their newborn as an ecstatic experience.

As mentioned in the previous chapter, midwives refer to these feelings of exaltation as "Superwomen Syndrome" and assert that they form the foundation for empowered parenting and successful breastfeeding. Empowerment is the expressed goal for each delivery, and midwives regard it as integral, and not secondary, to a "healthy mother and baby." Christina described her immediate postpartum experience this way: "When I saw her and held her, I knew what I had done. I had created a new life—a whole new person and I was overjoyed.... I mean I had birthed with no medications, no interventions and without anyone telling me what to do. I felt like I could do anything, which was good because parenting turned out to be very hard work!"

A sense of empowerment also contributed to the women's ability to resist the dominant paradigm of hospital care. Although participants viewed the source of their personal power differently, all agreed that power emanates from the acquisition of knowledge and the lived experience of birthing. Religious women were careful to explain that the ultimate source of power was their relationship with God and not something that they discovered inside themselves. For others, empowered birthing meant finding one's internal power. In either case, when women choose to give birth at home with midwives, they see themselves as effectively resisting unnecessary and harmful medical surveillance and manipulation. Kara, a participant who had delivered both of her children at home, explained: "After my homebirths, I just do not believe that women need all of these interventions or that 30 percent of us cannot get our babies out vaginally. I can see now that it is more about controlling women and maintaining the hospital as an institution. Do they even realize that they are beating us down, disempowering many of us in the process? If they did know, would they care?" Such explicit critiques of underlying power relations, combined with the overt refusal to work within established institutions, make homebirth not simply a birthing choice but also an act of resistance.

Power as Healing

Women who spoke of their homebirths as empowering relative to their previous experiences with hospital deliveries also claimed that the power of giving birth at home healed the scars of past "medical abuses." Marilyn, a participant who successfully completed a vaginal birth at home after a previous cesarean delivery, reflected on her experiences:

> I screwed around in support groups and counseling for two years over my c-section. I was so upset. I couldn't even close my eyes without remembering what it felt like—all of that pulling and tugging, knowing my insides were open and that my baby was being cut out of me. I had a nagging feeling even then that I just needed more time and that I could do it if they supported me.... Anyway, after the first few weeks

of grieving the experience, people lost their sympathy and were like: "Well, you have a healthy baby. You need to get over this." And let me tell you I tried.... But I had no outlet for that anger, that feeling of violation.... So, when I got pregnant again, there was no question for me. I wanted a midwife and a homebirth ... I delivered at home after a four-hour labor and 20 minutes of pushing that I loved every second of.... My home-born baby was also a full pound and a half bigger than my c-section baby. And the doctor had said my pelvis was inadequate. Whatever! I can tell you this. That birth healed me. It redeemed me ... I got my power back and I felt nothing but triumph.

The acquisition of knowledge as power combined with the lived experience of birth at home with midwives caused some mothers to replace "blind faith" in modern obstetrics with anger and resentment toward the "unnecessary interventions" of hospital deliveries. In comparing her hospital birth to her home delivery, Peg said:

I distinctly remember in my hospital birth saying many times that I didn't want drugs. I even wrote it in my birth plan, which I am convinced the nurse threw in the garbage can without reading.... At one point, I looked over and saw the nurse injecting this drug into my IV. She said I was being too noisy, which is totally what you do when you have something that big forcing its way out of you.... It [the drug] didn't help my pain. It just made be feel groggy and inarticulate (pause), powerless. I couldn't clearly state what I wanted because I was (sound like slurring words). I still don't know why that made me so mad, but it did. I realized I had no control.... My homebirth was so healing for me because I was totally with it. I could speak and say what I wanted and yell if I wanted to, and the midwives supported me. They really listened to me. I respect my body, my midwives, my instincts, but doctors, nurses, and drugs? Not so much now.

REJECTING "INTIMATE STRANGERS" IN THE BIRTHPLACE

A third conceptual category that emerged from homebirth narratives involved discussions of the value of intimacy and connectedness during prenatal, birth, and postpartum care. In explaining why they chose home over the hospital, many women emphasized the desire for intimacy that they believed was lacking in the hospital. In expressing their desire for intimacy these women articulated three distinct sub-themes: (1) intimacy as necessary for surrender; (2) birth as intimate/sexual; and (3) intimacy as a prerequisite for disclosure during the prenatal period. All of the women interviewed, with one exception, described the care they received as meeting and even exceeding their expectations for intimacy. They regarded the sense of connection produced in the birthplace as essential to the development of social support networks that would help sustain their new family, especially in the early months of parenting. The intimacy generated through the homebirth experience and the networking with other families often provided by midwives created a supportive space for women to expand their individual narratives into new, collective stories that presented an even stronger challenge to public hospital birth narratives. This "strength in numbers" plays a vital role in sustaining homebirth as a minority social movement.

Intimacy as Necessary for Surrender

The women I interviewed and attended in delivery view trust between mother and midwife as the "heart of midwifery care." It is "essential for a safe and empowering birth" as it enables mothers to feel "comfortable enough to surrender to the power of contractions." Participants explained that if they could establish a relationship of trust and intimacy with their care provider before labor's onset, they would then be better equipped to cope with the pain of labor. "Feeling safe" during the birth "releases fear," which they believe "makes the pain of labor more bearable." Rachel said, "Knowing I was safe, and that the pain didn't mean something was wrong, made it all manageable." These women view intimacy, trust, feeling safe, and the ability to surrender as intertwined and essential components of a successful birthing experience.

Many participants used the term *laborland* to help explain what happens when a woman and her attendant create a "safe, intimate, and trusting space." When a birthing mother is confident that "someone trustworthy is guarding her" and "watching out for her and her baby's well-being," she can "let down her guard," "hear her inner voice," and "fully surrender to birth." Laborland is a metaphysical place that midwives believe all (or almost all) mothers enter "to uncover the power to birth." It is located deep within each woman, though not all find it during labor because of the inhibiting effects of medications that dull pain and the "fear of letting go of the conscious mind." Midwives know that a mother is in laborland when she acquires "a far off look," "stops communicating during the contractions," and becomes "primal" (read intuitive) in her "birth song."

Participants who had experienced both home and hospital births emphasized the differences between attempting to deliver in the hospital under the watchful eyes of "intimate strangers" and the sense of safety and the ability to surrender that came with knowing their care providers well. Many homebirthers also explicitly connected the decrease in the number of "distance-producing interventions" and technologies used during their deliveries at home with the production of intimacy and their consequent ability to surrender to labor. Participants most commonly mentioned electronic fetal monitoring as an example of a distance-producing technology standard in hospitals. This technology allows nurses and doctors to monitor fetal heart rates for several patients at the same time on computer screens at the nurses' station. In home deliveries, as discussed in Chapter 3, midwives use a handheld ultrasound device called a Doppler to monitor the baby's well-being as reflected by the pattern of the fetal heartbeat. The midwife, unlike hospital practitioners, must be in the room and right next to the mother in order to monitor. Because women are not continuously connected to a machine, they also tend to feel less encumbered. As Sophie explained:

> My midwife told me about the importance of getting out of my conscious mind, letting go and surrendering to birth. I know what she means now after having my third baby at home.... It was dark and quiet except for the sounds of my birth song and the heart tones, and I felt so safe. For me, birth feels like a "back of the cave" experience, almost like I need to be inside a womb of safety myself, and that kind of intimacy is what I got at home.... In the hospital you cannot go there, at least I couldn't. I mean just all the asking you what you're allergic to and that automatic blood pressure cuff thing, that monitor and then the IV pole. You cannot just let go when you are attached to so many tubes. You really have to think OK, what is attached to me where, and how can I get over there without yanking something out?

Birth as Sexual/Intimate

Some of the women who discussed the importance of intimacy and trust as prerequisites for surrender explicitly made a connection to the second sub-theme in intimacy narratives—birth as sexual/intimate. Gwen, who had experienced one hospital birth and two home births, explained that just as she would have had difficulty engaging in sexual intercourse with strangers looking on, so she felt the need go into labor in the presence of people with an intimate connection to her:

> Birth is a really sexual thing you know. I mean it's the same hormones. And listen to the sounds you make when you're laboring—it sounds like sex! For me it was so like that ... you know how if you're having sex and someone just barges in or even if they knock and come in quietly, you really get out of your rhythm? (laughing) It's pretty much over until you can get the mood back. Well, that was sort of how my hospital birth was for me. I would get this great labor pattern going and then every time they came in to check me or poke around, it was gone. It was an uphill battle ... but at home I knew the midwives were close by watching over us. They made this really intimate space where I could just contract and moan and push and do my thing.

Intimacy as a Prerequisite for Disclosure

Women who discussed the value of intimacy, trust, or connectedness with care providers also explained that as they got to know their midwives well, they were more likely to disclose information pertinent to their care. In telling her home-birth story, Vikki shared how she had experienced extreme cravings for potting

soil and coffee grounds during her pregnancies, a phenomenon known as pica.[1]
Vikki had not felt comfortable telling her obstetrician about these cravings, but
she shared them willingly with her midwife because she felt they had a "more
equal relationship" and that she was less likely to be judged:

> I told her about my craving and she was so amazing about it. She said:
> "Isn't it really cool how our bodies let us know when we are missing
> something we need?" She said my cravings were my body's way of
> letting me know I needed more of some specific nutrient and that it was
> probably iron I was lacking. She got me on these liquid vitamins and
> sure enough—no more cravings.

Anthropologist Robbie Davis-Floyd, in her analyses of American birthing
models (1992, 1994a, 1994b), has focused on connectedness and intimacy as
one the most fundamental values underlying midwives' more holistic approach
to birth. This connectedness, she explains, exists in opposition to the medical
model of birth that is predicated upon separation—separation of "milk from
breasts, mothers from babies, fetuses from pregnancies, sexuality from procre-
ation and pregnancy from motherhood."[2] "The warm exchange of breath and
sweat, of touch and gaze, of body oils and emotions, that characterizes births in
which there is intimate connection between the mother and her caretaker has
given way in the United States to the cool penetration of needles, the distant
interpretation of lines on a graph" (Davis-Floyd & Davis, 1997, p. 315). Like
the midwives who attend them, participants in this study place value on interper-
sonal connections and intimacy. As Grace explained, "I'll take the pain, the
power, the pleasure, the intimacy of an unmedicated birth over an epidural any
day. I didn't want a sterile, white-washed, 'Oprah on the television in the background' birth, thank you very much!"

The intimacy experienced and valued as essential in homebirth stories affirms
and sustains individual narratives even in the face of social sanctioning and ostracism. The sense of connection through common cause and shared experience
provided in homebirth networks further facilitates the development of alternative, public narratives. This social support enables women to face detractors and
often to become articulate and outspoken critics of the unequal power relations
and "obstetric abuses" that they find still plague medical models of birth today.
Women also provide each other support through online communities. Kelly said,

> After I go visit my parents and listen to them joking about how
> "out there" I am, you know because of the homebirth and the fact
> that I plan to nurse him for two years and we use a sling and on and
> on … I have to go back home and reconnect to my community,

---

1. Pica is a craving for substances not normally considered food items such as dirt, ice
chips, and laundry starch. See Wiley and Katz (1998) for an overview of anthropological
perspectives on dietary cravings in pregnancy.

2. Excerpt from Barbara Katz Rothman's Plenary Address, Midwives' Alliance of North
America Conference, New York City, November 1992, as cited by Davis-Floyd and
Davis (1997, p. 315).

so I don't feel like I'm crazy or a bad mother. I know what I'm doing is right for me and my baby, but sometimes the cultural pressure is just too much to handle alone.

The intimacy developed in support groups builds on the sense of connection experienced during the delivery and plays a role in keeping women's individual and collective counter-narratives from being completely subsumed by the power of mainstream obstetric meta-narratives and discourses.

INTERIOR DECORATING OBSTETRICS

In response to consumer demands for more humane birthing practices, many hospitals in the United States now offer birthing rooms with floral wallpaper, wooden beds, lovely cabinets that hide medical equipment until the time of delivery, and champagne and lobster dinners for postpartum celebrations. Women who choose to give birth at home with midwives expressly reject these attempts to create more homelike and less institutionalized environments in the hospital, often referring to them as "superficial efforts," or as one woman put it, "interior decorating obstetrics." They regard such changes as façades used to cover up the underlying belief of the medical establishment—that women are incapable of birthing without obstetric management. They also view these changes as superficial, vastly insufficient, and even insulting because they "trick women into thinking they represent a more woman-centered or holistic approach to birth." Participants pointed out that in the United States, cesarean-section rates have continued to rise each year, even while modifications have given hospital rooms a more family-friendly atmosphere. Homebirthers call instead for the comprehensive reform of an obstetric establishment they view as overly expensive, intrusive, and disempowering.

SUMMARY AND CONCLUSION

An examination of themes grounded in women's homebirth narratives and analyzed from the perspective of Critical Medical Anthropology reveal three integrated concepts: knowledge, power, and intimacy. These themes help to explain the processes and motivations involved when women bypass mainstream obstetric care and give birth at home with midwives. Findings suggest that women often begin with a process of unlearning and relearning, where they acquire new knowledge and consequently begin to question the validity of mainstream public and meta-narratives. As they come to value alternative forms of authoritative knowledge that include embodied and intuitive ways of knowing, mothers reject physicians as the sole experts in the birthplace. When women adopt more egalitarian forms of knowledge sharing and production, they contribute to unmasking covert sources of power at play in medical birth settings.

The development of individual and collective narratives helps to reconcile disparities between dominant meta-narratives and women's lived experiences of pregnancy and birth, and often stimulates a transition from faith in doctors and hospitals to faith in birthing bodies, babies, and midwives. As women move into the domain of direct action, their critiques of the medical model of birth are embodied in the lived experience of delivering at home. Personal power, agency, and, for some women, the healing they experience as they are transformed by the power of unmedicated delivery further affirm their belief in, and advocacy of, new public narratives. These narratives embrace a reality where women's bodies function exquisitely despite the absence of major technological interventions.

Homebirth is associated with intimacy between midwife and mother, mother and baby, and mother and partner/family. This sense of intimacy and connectedness often extends to encompass larger homebirth support networks as women seek out other like-minded mothers, usually with the help of their midwives. Through network formation, women find strength in numbers, as well as a continued sense of connection that affirms and sustains new ways of seeing and living birth and early parenting. Social support also prevents the subversion of their views by the power of institutionalized birthing models and social pressures for conformity.

Finally, women's homebirth narratives suggest a linearity of process that, in reality, may not have moved smoothly from start to finish as described above. As women attempt to make sense of their experiences through storytelling, they order and structure events according to a chronology that does not necessarily reflect the progression of events and processes as they were actually lived. The motivations and personal journeys that women express in their homebirth narratives are ongoing processes—ones they revisit continually as they face new detractors and work to embrace, voice, and live homebirth as an act of resistance.

Chapter 5

Toward a (R)evolutionary Obstetrics
"Normal" Birth in Homebirth and Evolutionary Perspective

In a warm, candle-lit room in the early hours of the morning, Amanda moans and gently sways her hips as she leans over the edge of the inflatable birthing pool. Her husband and I each grasp a hand and offer soft words of encouragement. Her other children, ranging in ages from eight to two years old, gather together around the edges of the tub, watching quietly as they wait for their baby sister to be born. Lucinda monitors fetal heart tones and charts the progress of the labor. As the contractions strengthen, Amanda's moans intensify: "I can't. I can't. The pain, it's all in my back. I can't take it anymore." Lucinda reassures: "You can. You are! The baby will rotate once you bring her down a little farther. You're almost there. Don't give up. You can do this. Keep pushing."

As the head inches down, an enormous contraction grips Amanda's belly and rotates the baby through the final position change required to navigate the pelvic bones and emerge. This last-minute adjustment of the baby's head removes any obstacle, and I quickly guide the mother's hands down so she can feel the head. "That's your baby. She's right there. Amanda, breathe with me, she's coming now, gentle pushes, gentle, gentle. Let your body do it, slowly, slowly. Good." Eyes locked,

midwives and father guide the newest member of the family out and into her mother's hands. The other children sit mesmerized, breathless with excitement as Amanda tenderly lifts baby Soriah out of the water and holds her to her chest. Quiet tears begin to fall. The strength, the joy, and the power of new life fill the room and forever set this morning apart as one that even the youngest members of this family are unlikely to forget. Once again, I reflect back on a day's work, amazed at the power and the intensity of women giving birth.
—Field notes, June 2003

T he intimacy of homebirth care allows mothers and midwives to develop relationships of deep trust and affection. In almost all cases, homebirth midwives commit to attend a particular woman, agreeing to care for her whenever she goes into labor, and not just if she happens to be the midwife "on call" when labor begins. In addition, midwives conduct all prenatal visits and begin "labor sitting" as soon as the mother requests the midwife's presence. The closeness and depth of knowing that develop out of this approach means that midwives are often intimately acquainted with the physiological, emotional, and social nuances of individual mothers and babies. They carry a depth of knowledge that comes from attending a small number of women in a continuous, individualized, and time-intensive manner, and this, midwives assert, makes them better able to identify complications or deviations from normal. Conventional obstetric care tends to be fragmented with several physicians in one practice conducting prenatal visits and sharing call. Midwives believe that obstetricians are in danger of letting the details of an individual mother's pregnancy "slip through the cracks."

Midwives who practice at home must always be concerned with safety and monitoring so they can help to judge when a transport to the hospital is required. They are focused on supporting normal birth whenever possible, and their understanding of the range of normal for pregnant and birthing mothers is what allows them to respond quickly and effectively to abnormal patterns and complications. Because medical authorities do not regard them as legitimate providers, the knowledge and experience of homebirth midwives are notably absent in debates over what constitutes "normal," and by extension "abnormal," birthing patterns. In this chapter, I discuss midwives' views of normal birth, the practices they use to help ensure "that births stay normal," and the clinical consequences of these approaches as measured by their associated outcomes.

As we will see, the models and practices employed by homebirth midwives provide new ways of thinking about and approaching childbirth that, when analyzed with their clinical outcomes, indicate ways we can begin to re-envision widely critiqued technocratic, obstetric approaches. Homebirth outcomes are free of physician-effect—the impact of obstetricians' belief systems, training, and management styles on outcomes—and laden with midwife-effects. The examination of childbirth outcomes that result from different models of care allows us to see how birth can unfold when the administrators and overseers of deliveries adhere to different explanatory models of childbearing. Since they are unmedicated and free from most of the new technologies that dominate hospital-birthing protocols, homebirths are among the few remaining places researchers can look to try to understand what constitutes "normal" human delivery patterns. How do homebirth midwives define normal and abnormal in birth? How do they act on this knowledge? How does their assessment of normal affect their mode of care? And what maternal and infant health outcomes result from their approaches?

Discussions of what is normal in human birth, and what is abnormal or dangerous, have several disparate perspectives. The first, what we have been calling the medical or technocratic model of care, is held by many obstetricians who either consciously or unconsciously subscribe to a view of birth as abnormal and as a potentially dangerous experience for women and babies. As a result, they feel most comfortable when they can medicate and manage it in the controlled environment of a hospital. A second view adhered to by some feminist researchers (Walrath 2003, 2006) and many natural birth advocates sees birth as a natural, healthy process that does not, as a rule, require medical intervention. According to this view, culture and patriarchy have made women fear birth, robbing them of agency and personal power in the birthplace. In desiring to empower women by overturning assumptions about the dysfunctional, pathological, or maladapted nature of the female birthing body, they may overstate the case for viewing birth as a normal process. As Lucinda, a midwife who is critical of this stance, is fond of saying, "Birth is natural, but so is death. Sometimes we don't want a completely natural outcome!"

Somewhere between the extremes of the "birth is dangerous and belongs in the hospital" and the "birth is natural and doesn't require a hospital" perspectives lie other possibilities. By examining homebirth midwives' knowledge, practices, and outcomes through the lens of a relatively new approach in medical anthropology called evolutionary medicine, a more nuanced view of "normal birth" emerges. Midwives see many human birth patterns as normal while identifying others as abnormal and in need of medical intervention. Practical experience providing care enables them, over time, to define a clear view of normal and to distinguish between births that carry low risk and those that carry high risk. Midwives' perspectives developed through the frequent exposure to successful, unmedicated home deliveries, punctuated by the rare life-and-death judgments they make, have much to contribute to debates over what constitutes normal birth. In this chapter, I begin with an overview of evolutionary medicine, discussing its role in structuring recent debates about what constitutes normal birth in humans, and then move on to present the perspectives and health outcomes of homebirth midwives within this debate. It is my hope that homebirth midwives will be able to influence the academic discussion on this issue.

EVOLUTIONARY MEDICINE AND THE "NORMAL BIRTH" DEBATE

Evolutionary medicine—an emerging subfield of medical anthropology—is founded on the assumption that most contemporary illnesses result from incompatibilities or discordances between the environments under which humans evolved and those associated with industrializing societies (Trevathan, Smith, & McKenna, 2008). Only 1–2 percent of our biological make-up has evolved since the ape-human split occurred between five and seven million years ago, and this means that the vast majority of our genes are ancient in origin. As a species, we have experienced a few simple genetic changes since the agricultural revolution 12,000 years ago, but the pace of cultural evolution is generally much faster than biological evolution. As a result, humans today occupy 35,000-year-old model bodies that are not particularly well adapted to the technocratic and industrializing cultures many of us live in (Armelagos, Brown, & Turner, 2005; Eaton, Eaton, & Cordain, 2002).

We often encounter significant mismatches between contemporary behaviors and health practices and the ancient, biocultural adaptations embedded in our bodies. Humans, for example, evolved under conditions where high-fat foods were simply not available and high levels of exercise were a given. Hundreds of thousands of years of selective pressures under these conditions shaped human biology, leaving us without effective adaptations for the pervasive fast food and sedentary desk jobs that characterize contemporary society. High rates of obesity and heart disease result, as humans move further from the ancestral condition in response to cultural and environmental changes. The notion that discontinuities between the conditions under which humans evolved and the conditions we live in today produce disease is called the "discordance hypothesis," and it forms the foundation for evolutionary medicine.

Researchers who adhere to this approach attempt to propose evolutionary solutions and treatments to resolve discordances (Stearns, Nesse, & Haig, 2008). By examining stressors in the physical and social environment and how humans respond to them, researchers and clinicians gain a more contextualized understanding of human health patterns that move beyond individual afflictions and their immediate symptoms (Crews & Gerber, 2008). What can an evolutionary medicine approach tell us about normal birth for humans and, by extension, how we might we treat birth in a way that works with, rather than against, our evolved biology?

The unique anatomical characteristics of the human pelvis and the resulting complexity of our delivery mechanisms have been discussed extensively since Wilton Krogman (1951) first referred to childbirth as a "scar of human evolution." The tendency to see birth as difficult and precariously adapted in humans relative to other mammals stems from what evolutionary biologists call the "obstetrical dilemma." This dilemma refers to the two conflicting selective pressures that have shaped the human pelvis over time—upright walking and childbirth. The human pelvis must be relatively wide side-to-side and flattened front-to-back to accommodate the muscular attachments needed for upright or "bipedal" walking. However, the pelvis must also be relatively open, rounded, and spacious to allow for the passage of a large-brained infant. These competing selective pressures result in an obstetrical compromise where birth is complicated, painful, and usually a tight fit.

Unlike most of our primate relatives whose infants follow a straight shot out of an ample pelvis (see Figure 5.1), human babies must maneuver through a series of complex orientations, called the "mechanisms of labor," to navigate the changing diameters of the birth canal (see Figure 5.2). The baby's head enters the mother's pelvis facing to the side, looking toward the mother's hip. As the head descends through the pelvis, it rotates so that the back of the baby's head turns and rests against the mother's front. The baby then begins to flex the chin toward the chest. This process allows the smallest diameter of the fetal head to be born first. As the uterus continues to contract and the mother pushes, the back of the baby's head becomes visible at the opening of the birth canal; this stage is called "crowning." The mother continues to push, and more and more of the head becomes visible, until gradually the baby extends the neck and the face sweeps across the floor of the vaginal opening. Higher up, the shoulders begin the same set of rotations the head navigated minutes or hours before. Once the shoulders pass through the same twists and turns, the top shoulder emerges. Next the baby's body bends upward allowing the bottom shoulder to be born. Once the shoulders have cleared, the rest of the body tends to pop out quickly,

FIGURE 5.1 Solitary, forward facing delivery in nonhuman primates (illustration by Marie Le Glatin Keis).

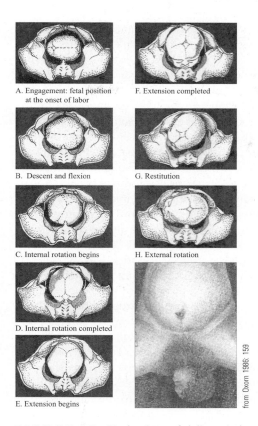

A. Engagement: fetal position
  at the onset of labor

F. Extension completed

B. Descent and flexion

G. Restitution

C. Internal rotation begins

H. External rotation

D. Internal rotation completed

E. Extension begins

from Oxorn 1986: 159

FIGURE 5.2   Mechanisms of delivery in humans with backward facing emergence
(illustration by Marie Le Glatin Keis, adapted from Oxorn-Foote Human Labor and
Birth, 3rd Edition. Appleton-Century-Crofts, 1986).

and this is another reason why midwives say they "catch" babies. Many of these
complicated maneuvers are visible from the outside, and they are fascinating to
watch. As a result of this physiology, evolutionary biologists, with few exceptions, view human birth as significantly more dangerous, of longer duration,
and substantially more painful than that of other mammals.

The comparatively difficult nature of childbirth in our species has lead to
unique birthing behaviors. For example, most other mammals, including all nonhuman primates, go off by themselves to a dark, enclosed, and quiet space to
give birth alone, whereas human mothers almost always seek company and assistance from people they know well—female relatives, friends, and experienced
birth attendants. At some point in human history, the benefits of assistance at
birth must have outweighed the safety of delivering alone under the cover of
night. Cross-cultural evidence supports the notion that assisted birth is normal
for humans, because very few societies idealize unassisted birth, and in those
that do, solitary birth tends to be the norm only for women who have already
had one baby successfully. The Kalahari desert-dwelling Ju/'hoansi, for example,

highly value unassisted birth, though not all women actually achieve this cultural ideal. First-time mothers or mothers with a history of difficult deliveries usually give birth surrounded by female relatives and friends (Konner & Shostack, 1987; Shostack, 1981), though unassisted births do occur and, even today, remain an important means of "proving oneself" (Biesele, 1997). The vast majority of cultures around the world, however, make some provision for assistance at birth.

This unique human condition of assisted delivery has been termed "obligate midwifery" (Trevathan, 1997), and it likely evolved in humans because of three important differences in the birth process. First, human babies almost always emerge facing backward—that is, with the their backs facing their mother's front. As a result, birthing mothers have difficulty reaching down, as nonhuman primates do, and gently guiding the baby out, wiping the infant's airway clean with their hands or mouth, and removing the umbilical cord from around the neck when necessary. Second, modern humans give birth to infants who require extensive care from the time of delivery because they are so immature at birth. A baby giraffe can get up and follow its mother around soon after delivery, whereas human babies remain relatively helpless for months. The infant's helplessness may be a second reason why extra hands at a birth contribute to better reproductive success, especially when mothers are exhausted by long and arduous labors. Third, powerful maternal emotions, including excitement, anxiety, fear, tension, and uncertainty, provide an evolutionary impetus for women to acquire support during labor and birth. The emotions of childbirth that encourage a laboring mother to seek assistance and companionship are likely behavioral adaptations to the pain and difficulty resulting from the obstetrical dilemma. Taken together, these three unique characteristics of human birth may have contributed to the transformation of the birthing process from a solitary to a highly social enterprise, setting humans on a trajectory toward social and cultural interventions in birth (Rosenberg, 1992; Trevathan, 1997). From the perspective of evolutionary medicine, the question now becomes: What kinds of social and cultural interventions are most effective?

In 2003, a medical anthropologist named Dana Walrath published an article aimed at exposing the roles of cultural perception and political power behind contemporary models of human childbirth. She challenges some of our most fundamental assumptions regarding childbirth in *Homo sapiens* and asserts that concepts such as the obstetrical dilemma and obligate midwifery have lead the medical establishment to rely too heavily on technocratic models of care. She sees this framework as a slippery slope toward viewing all births as potentially pathological and, by implication, abnormal. Walrath questions whether the mechanisms of delivery in humans with backward-facing emergence—which, remember, supposedly necessitates an attendant and obligate midwifery—are the only patterns of delivery that should be considered normal in humans. She believes that human birth mechanisms vary today and probably did so in the past, to a greater extent than the singular norm of backward-facing emergence suggests. Perhaps the assumed difficulty of human birth and this singular mechanism of delivery attributed to the obstetrical dilemma and requiring obligate midwifery are simply products of male-biased research and evidence of the tendency for biomedicine and paleo-anthropology to pathologize female reproductive processes.

These questions about what constitutes normal birth are not just academic. They are of vital clinical importance because they guide whether doctors or midwives simply observe and wait or intervene to treat complications. Today, the most common reason given for medical interventions such as cesarean sections is the slowing of labor caused by so-called malpresentations of the fetus. Babies that attempt to emerge feet first or head first, but forward facing, rather than backward facing, are the prime targets for surgical intervention and almost single-handedly explain the rise in cesarean-section rates that in the United States now exceed recommended levels by between 200 and 300 percent (Althabe & Belizan, 2006). Surgical deliveries result in maternal deaths three times more frequently than do vaginal deliveries, and thus, it is essential that we develop a better understanding of when to intervene and when to allow a birth to unfold on its own.

Should mechanisms of delivery besides backward facing be considered normal for humans? Should forward-facing presentations, so common in nonhuman primates, be considered a variation of normal and indicative of multiple mechanisms of delivery in humans? Or are they abnormal, problematic "malpresentations" as the medical model refers to them? The clinical tolerance of obstetricians for variation in birthing patterns, as well as for the length of labor, has declined dramatically in the last 50 years. Today only backward-facing infants are considered normal, and the length of normal labor in first-time mothers has been cut from 24 to 12 hours (Davis-Floyd, 2004). The routinization of cesarean section and a narrowing window for what is considered clinically acceptable have at least partially contributed to the unprecedented surgical delivery rate and poorer-than-expected maternal and infant health outcomes discussed in Chapter 1. Questions like these test the very relevance of contemporary medical anthropology.

HONORING MIDWIVES' KNOWLEDGE: THE EXPLANATORY POWER OF LIVED EXPERIENCE

The examination of maternal–child health outcomes associated with diverse approaches to birthing care provide a range of possibilities and interpretations, as opposed to the uncritical acceptance of a singular model of "high-tech" hospital birth as the only appropriate solution to the obstetric dilemma. During my fieldwork with midwives, I observed how they viewed and reacted to each delivery, using my observations to make inferences about how they were defining normal birth. In addition, I asked midwives in the Midwest, and later in Oregon, to explain what they considered to be normal and abnormal in birth. Several common themes emerged that have much to contribute to academic debates over what constitutes normal birth. I discuss three here: (1) midwives' acceptance of a wide range of normal for length of labor and the pushing stage; (2) the focus on prevention of forward-facing infants through exercise promotion and a practice called "optimal fetal positioning"; and (3) when prevention fails, the time-honored, hands-on, and "low-tech" labor interventions midwives use to help to correct complications.

"It's Not a Problem Unless It's a Problem": Length
of Labor and the Pushing Stage

Homebirth midwives, as a rule, believe that the range of normal for the length of labor and the pushing stage is much broader than that currently promoted in medical models of birth. Because ranges of normal are so wide from midwives' perspectives, they believe that caring for a woman in labor requires flexibility and highly individualized assessment and support. Lucinda explained it this way: "The medical establishment puts restrictions on the timing of labor and delivery that are too narrow and too one-size-fits-all. I can tell you from attending over 1,000 unmedicated deliveries that birth doesn't unfold according to any means or averages! What is normal for one woman may not be so for another, so I don't use arbitrary numbers to decide if something is OK or if I need to intervene. If a mother is pushing longer than average, I say: 'so what?' As long as mother and baby are fine, we keep going. It's not a problem unless it's a problem."

Lucinda's "arbitrary numbers" comment is a reference to Friedman's labor curve that has been a part of hospital birthing culture since the late 1950s. As discussed in Chapter 2, Friedman's labor curve is used to evaluate the rate of dilation and descent of the baby through the birth canal. Obstetricians often view women who take longer than average for this curve as requiring an intervention, such as IV pitocin or surgery, to speed delivery. Homebirth midwives tend to ignore the standards set by Friedman's curve along with other duration guidelines used by hospitals. Moreover, they lack the medications required to speed up a labor even if they think it might be desirable. Homebirth outcomes are, thus, an exciting place to look to see what happens when midwives operate according to wider ranges of normal for labor and pushing lengths. During my fieldwork in the Midwest midwifery practice, I collected information on labor and pushing lengths for 602 cases, from 15 years of client charts, to determine if midwives were operationalizing a different view of normal. Indeed, I found that the midwives were acknowledging, and treating as normal, labor and pushing lengths that are significantly longer than those advocated for by the Friedman's curve (see Table 5.1). These numbers confirm that midwives accept a truly enormous range of normal. I had made the same discovery through participant observation just a few days into my fieldwork.

It was late December, and the first terrible snowstorm of the season was forecasted for that evening. Just before the first flurries began to fall, we were called to Anna's house where she had been laboring for about 12 hours with only her family present and was ready for additional support. The midwives arrived, assessed mother and baby, and started massaging Anna's back through contractions that were now coming very close together. Anna labored clinging to her sisters and husband, periodically encouraging all within earshot to believe in her and not to give up on her. Anna's baby was forward facing, instead of backward facing, and this was causing terrible back pain, along with excruciatingly slow labor progress. The midwives calmly monitored heart tones that never wavered, encouraging Anna to walk and change positions frequently to help the baby into a backward facing position. The snow fell deeper and deeper.

T A B L E   5.1   Variation in Labor and Pushing Duration Between the Midwest (MW) Sample and the Friedman's Curve (1955, 1967), Measured in Minutes

1st time mothers	MW Sample		Friedman (1955, 1967)	
	Active Labor	Pushing	Active Labor	Pushing
No.	n = 61	n = 81	n = 500	
Mean	376.41	96.98	276	66
SD	253.879	82.342	216	48
Median	310.00	72.00	198	33.0
95th percentile	1014.00	290.10	702	174
Range	1155	347	*	*

2nd time or > mothers	MW Sample		Friedman (1955, 1967)	
	Active Labor	Pushing	Active Labor	Pushing
No.	n = 218	n = 359	n = 500	
Mean	278.21	30.41	144	23.4
SD	198.726	47.702	132	18
Median	230.50	18.00	192	8.5
95th percentile	696.70	99.00	312	66
Range	1121	673	*	*

*Values not reported.

Almost 60 hours later, the baby had not delivered. Although all vital signs were still normal, Anna was exhausted. Transport was not a viable option due to the weather conditions, and remarkably, Anna still felt she had it in her to continue. She had made it to 9 centimeters, almost complete dilation, as the cervix generally needs to open to 10 centimeters before pushing can commence. Anna at one point asked what would happen if she just tried to push before complete dilation. Figuring there wasn't much to lose, Lucinda told Anna to give it a try. Ten minutes later, little baby Gabriel emerged perfectly healthy, pink, and screaming. Anna exclaimed: "Wow, that was fast!" "Well, not really," said Lucinda, "but we are so glad he is here!"

Six months later I was sitting in my kitchen having coffee when the phone rang. I picked it up and heard the slightly panicked voice of Lori, a woman planning her fifth baby with Miriam. She said, "Hi Missy, I think that I might have had a contraction. I'm just telling you because you said this baby could come faster than the others and (pause) um, oh, I think my water just broke and uhhhhhhhhhhh (pushing sound). Then, high-pitched and nearly hysterical, Paaaaaaaaul!" (Sound of the phone hitting the floor, fumbling.) I'm grabbing my keys and birth bag and running for the door. More screaming and pushing sounds. Then … total silence for a few seconds and the cry of a healthy new-born. Paul picked up the phone and said, "Um, um, um, we have a baby. We have a baby!" I said, "I know. I can hear her. Dry her off. Put her to the breast, and keep her warm. Don't do anything with the umbilical cord. We're on our way." When I hung up, the cell phone indicated that the entire labor and pushing, including my rushed postpartum instructions, had taken 3 minutes and 28 seconds! Miriam and I made it before the placenta delivered.

Is normal labor 72 hours long or 3 minutes and 28 seconds? The rest of my time as an apprentice taught me that it is usually somewhere in the middle, and that a relatively wide range of normal is associated with positive outcomes. Obstetricians are rarely able to have these kinds of experiences and to observe births like Anna's especially. Pressures from within the system to intervene are simply too great. In Anna's' case, she likely would have ended up with a cesarean, or a drug to speed labor, sometime after one day, two at the latest. Lori's case would have been a 911 call, after which mother and baby would have been whisked off to the emergency room for evaluation. They would have been seen as lucky, having narrowly escaped potential disaster. Physicians caring for women under relatively strict hospital protocols and seeking to avoid litigation simply do not have the opportunity to observe the range of normal I was privy to during my fieldwork and training.

The same wide range of normal guides my practice today as a homebirth midwife. I have been called to births in the middle of the night and returned back home before my husband was up for work. I have also been gone for days. I never know ahead of the call. Even after so many deliveries, birth continues to teach me about its incredible range of normal. In so many ways, normal is simply what we are used to.

"Guardians of Normal Birth": Holistic
Prevention over Intervention

All of the study participants and midwives I interviewed mentioned a second theme relevant for defining normal birth—the importance of holistic prevention over intervention. Midwives advocate a model of prenatal care that focuses on the prevention of complications and, by extension, minimizing the need for "high-tech" medical interventions at the time of delivery. Midwives report an extensive array of preventative strategies that together promote "holistically healthy" mothers and babies who are more likely to avoid complications and, thus, avoid transports to hospitals for invasive procedures. Midwives often describe their primary role as "guides on a journey," "trained companions" to a birthing mother, and "guardians of normal birth." Their job is to "keep a pregnancy and birth normal," to "keep a mother and baby as healthy as possible along the way," and "to intervene before something becomes a true problem." Midwives point out that they have a relatively limited range of technological interventions available to them at home and consequently are concerned with prevention and optimal health to a greater degree than most obstetricians. Lucinda explained:

> If you get a baby presenting in a less than optimal position in the hospital and a mother who is exhausted from a long labor as a result, they [the hospital staff] can just hook them up to machines, augment the labor, pull a baby out with a vacuum extractor, or even cut her open and deliver the baby that way. We see those things as extreme and overused, but occasionally necessary. Doctors do them too flippantly without thinking about the whole woman and how she is going to feel for the next six weeks or even the rest of her life. Women don't forget their birth experiences. We don't want it to get to the point where those things are necessary, and so we're moving to keep things normal all the time.

This emphasis on avoiding complications leads many midwives to embrace what they describe as a more proactive role in prevention—what some called a more "hands-on" approach during the prenatal period. Miriam said:

> If we're working with a mother whose baby is breech at eight months, we're not just going to wait to see if the baby moves into a head down and anterior [backward facing] position. We are going to want to encourage the baby to get into a better position. It's true that if we leave things alone, the baby could move anyway, but if he or she doesn't, then the mom may be facing a cesarean. We want to prevent complications whenever possible and not just to monitor them until a more extensive intervention is necessary. It's about keeping things normal.

Many of the preventative practices used by homebirth midwives to encourage "good outcomes," "normal birth," and "optimized health" revolve around the promotion of lifestyle changes that include an emphasis on a balanced, whole-foods diet low in refined sugars; the encouragement of daily exercise; support for avoiding or reducing smoking; and prenatal mind-body integration activities such as yoga or meditation. As discussed in Chapter 4, prenatal education and empowerment through discussing mothers' questions and concerns at length and encouraging women repeatedly at every visit about their body's ability to give birth are central prenatal care strategies. Midwives espouse a strong ethic of loving and nurturing the expectant mother, or "mothering the mother," as I have noted. Many of them believe that mothering is an under-supported and undervalued enterprise in the United States, and as such, they regard the childbearing year as a time to compensate through giving intimate support to mothers and families. As Carmen frequently said, "Love is what gets the baby in, love is also what will get it out."

The homebirth midwifery focus on an integrated, comprehensive, and "whole woman" approach is consistent with what we know about obligate midwifery and the evolutionary impetus to seek support and companionship during delivery. Few midwives have ever heard of evolutionary medicine, but all have found through their own experience that technocratic models of birth vastly underestimate the emotional and psychosocial needs of women in labor. They work all through pregnancy to foster a close relationship with their clients that will make them feel safe, empowered, and "in good hands" once labor begins.

The implementation of standards of care designed to produce holistic and positive outcomes is central to the role of midwives as "guardians of normal birth." Victoria explained:

> I am the guardian of normal birth. I stay alert to signs that things might be going astray and then women often only need a small nudge to get back on track—a diet change, an herbal supplement, some exercises to optimize the position of the baby.... The medical establishment doesn't understand all the nuances of normal pregnancy and birth because they don't know their mothers and babies well enough. Their approaches are too aggressive. We nudge. They hit with a two-by-four!

Midwives agree that backward-facing positions are preferable because forward-facing ones often result in more painful and longer labors like the ones experienced by Amanda in the opening of this chapter and Anna during the snowstorm. As part of their commitment to the prevention of future complications and holistic care, beginning at 30 to 32 weeks into a pregnancy, midwives initiate a strategy they call "Optimal Fetal Positioning." Its goal is to encourage the baby to rest head down in the pelvis with the back facing toward the mother's front, as opposed to the back facing toward the mother's back. Midwives evaluate the position of the baby by massaging the mother's belly at every prenatal visit and listening to what women have to say about where they are feeling fetal movement. When mothers have babies in any position other than backward facing, midwives assign exercises that they say help to convert the fetus from the less-than-optimal forward-facing position to a backward-facing one (see Figure 5.3). Midwives also prescribe regular swimming and walking, as well as postural changes where mothers focus on sitting upright, squatting, and avoiding reclined positions to encourage babies to enter the pelvis in the preferred backward-facing position. However, they remain realistic and explain to their clients that these approaches do not always work and that many factors influence fetal positioning, including the size of the baby, the shape of the maternal pelvis, and the amount and vigorousness of exercise engaged in by the mother in the second and third trimesters.

Early in my field research I asked Lucinda why she spent so much time focusing on fetal positioning. Clearly frustrated with my ignorance, she said she would talk to me about it after I had observed several labors for backward- and forward-facing infants. Indeed, I needed little instruction on the benefits of optimal fetal positioning after attending only a handful of forward-facing labors, especially in first-time mothers. None of the midwives who participated in my research were familiar with the debates in academic journals about the obstetrical dilemma, obligate midwifery, or the physiological mechanisms of "normal" human delivery. Nor had they calculated statistics on their own birth outcomes, though they did prepare comprehensive charts so

Scott and Sutton 1996

F I G U R E 5.3 Optimal fetal positioning exercises used to convert the fetus to a backward facing presentation (Illustration by Marie Le Glatin Keis).

that they could provide individual clients with written records of their home-birth experiences. Midwives' interpretations of what constitutes "normal" birth were impressionistic and based on thousands of hours of observation and assistance at unmedicated, home deliveries. Midwives have learned from their experiences that forward-facing presentations result in longer, more painful labors and are more likely to lead to maternal exhaustion, fetal distress, hospital transport, and cesarean section. They see it as their duty to help women avoid these complications whenever possible.

In working to ensure that as many babies as possible present in a backward-facing position, homebirth midwives seem to be accepting a narrower range of "normal" than researchers and natural birth advocates who may be overstating the extent to which risky variations in the human physiology of birth should be considered normal. Though all midwife participants espouse a model that emphasizes childbirth as a natural, normal, healthy, and non-pathological part of the life span for most women, all agreed that forward-facing presentations, especially in first-time mothers, are potentially abnormal and should be prevented whenever possible.

"Tricks of the Trade": Time-Honored, Low-Tech Labor Interventions

What happens when a woman goes into labor intending to deliver at home, but finds that her baby is poorly positioned? First, midwives wait to see if it will actually be a problem. Some women may labor and deliver with no apparent obstruction from a forward-facing infant, while others may find themselves in labor for days rather than hours. Midwives say that the position of the infant matters less for women who have previously delivered a baby. Victoria told all of her repeat clients, "Position doesn't matter so much the second time around. Once something that big has come out of you, fetal position is less of an issue. Don't worry. Once you get hard contractions, the baby will just rotate into an anterior [backward-facing] position." My experiences as an apprentice were consistent with Victoria's observation. Sometimes our biggest problem with second-time mothers was getting to them on time, especially if they had experienced a long, hard first birth. The women often waited too long to call, and so we jokingly referred to these as "one-glove births" because we often arrived so late, we hardly had time to get our gloves on.

Once during my apprenticeship the call came when we were all in a movie theater. Lucinda stepped outside to answer the phone and then came running back inside to grab me. We broke the speed limit on our way to the birth. When we arrived, Karen was sitting in a recliner with her legs tightly crossed looking like a deer in the headlights. "I'm sorry. I'm sorry I called you so late. I need to puuuuuuuush!" One glove, no equipment, and five seconds later, out came baby Matilda, pink and wailing. After the placenta delivered and we had the mother and infant tidied up and in bed nursing, Karen told us that she had experienced mild contractions all afternoon that were painful mostly in her lower back. She reasoned that she had a long time to go as in her first birth, and so she did not call. Suddenly as she was leaning over to pick up her toddler, she felt the baby rotate and "thunk down" into her pelvis. Her thoughts changed immediately, and she knew she had probably waited too long. I began to think "one-glove births" were kind of nice. We never had much to clean up afterward because all of our emergency equipment stayed in the car!

First-time mothers often were not so lucky; forward-facing labors almost always meant that the labor would be longer and harder and might even result in a transport. In this situation, the midwives worked hard to get the birth back on track and to "make it normal again." Midwives have an impressive repertoire of time-honored interventions they call "tricks of the trade" used to help normalize labor. I found these interventions fascinating because so many of them are uniformly applied across cultures and are precisely those predicted by evolutionary medicine. For example, as discussed in Chapter 3, midwives strongly encourage upright movement during labor. Freedom of movement in labor is the norm cross-culturally, as well as in our closest living primate relatives. The notion that women should lie in bed with their movement hindered by tubes and devices is relatively recent and unusual (Trevathan, 1999).

Midwives also employ an impressive array of position changes and methods for manipulating the shape and size of the mother's pelvis. Midwives say, "If you can't change the position of the baby, try changing the position of the mother." By lunging, squatting, walking up and down the stairs, swaying side to side in what they call the "birth dance," and in assuming a hands and knees position, mothers and midwives can sometimes encourage rotation of the baby. Another popular intervention with the same goal of encouraging a backward-facing position is called the "hip squeeze." This strategy involves the mother squatting with two helpers on either side each linking an arm, while using their free hands to push on the laboring mother's hips. The helpers pull against each other for leverage, which allows them to put greater pressure on the mother's hips. The pushing action helps to enlarge the outlet of the pelvis and often gives a baby room to turn. When these interventions fail, midwives will sometimes attempt what is called an "internal rotation" where the midwife places two fingers inside the vagina feeling for the back of the baby's head. Between contractions when the uterus is relaxed, she presses the back of the baby's head up toward the mother's front, effectively moving the baby from forward facing to a backward-facing position. If all of these methods fail and the mother becomes exhausted or the fetus shows signs of initial distress, midwives recommend transport to the hospital for more aggressive, high-tech interventions. Midwives resist making this recommendation until all else fails because hospital procedures such as vacuum extraction and cesarean section carry their own substantial risks, and so, are seen as a last resort.

Midwives' views and practices are challenging definitions of normal birth in three areas. First, midwives accept much longer lengths of labor and pushing as normal, refusing what they see as arbitrary time constraints. In doing so, they intervene in the birth process less frequently and less intrusively than their obstetric colleagues. Second, midwives do not claim all variations in birth as normal. They work hard to avoid and to rectify forward-facing infants, an indication that they are acknowledging a smaller range of normal for fetal positioning. Third, homebirth midwives use low-tech interventions passed down by word of mouth through generations of their "mother" and "grandmother" midwives before they recommend transport to the hospital. The move from home to hospital contains an implied admission that a birth is no longer normal. The question that remains is the "so what?" of midwives' views of normal birth. If midwives define and respond to normal and abnormal births in the ways I have described, what outcomes can we expect for the mothers and babies under their care?

HOMEBIRTH MIDWIFERY OUTCOMES

Midwives perspectives and practices as shaped by their concepts of normal birth have real and measurable effects on mothers and babies. In this section we examine these effects. We know from previous chapters that the vast majority of homebirth clients emerge feeling elated and empowered by their birth experiences. In the terminology of medical anthropology, they have excellent "psychosocial" outcomes. But how do mothers and babies fare clinically when they choose homebirth care? To answer this question, I examined the labor and delivery records from the Midwest practice, entering variables for the key indicators of maternal and infant well-being reported each year through the National Center for Health Statistics and in several large-scale studies on birth safety. This enabled me to evaluate how homebirthing mothers and babies in this sample do relative to the national average, as well as to published studies on hospital birth. Table 5.2 summarizes these findings.

In 2005, two years after I completed my apprenticeship, I returned to the Midwest to share my research findings with study participants, the midwives who trained me, and interested members of the public. The venue was a large room at a local university that had facilitated my fieldwork. As the time for the talk approached, the room filled to capacity with mothers, babies, midwives, and academics. Earlier I had told the midwives not to worry, that their outcomes were good but that I would not unveil specific results until I returned to their community to make a formal presentation. As the lights dimmed and the PowerPoint presentation was projected onto the auditorium's screen, the air was full of tension, and I was aware, once again, of how much was at stake for midwives and their clients in the audience. As practitioners in a state that does not legally protect a woman's right to homebirth with a midwife, midwives care for their clients at enormous personal risk. During my apprenticeship I had seen a midwife's backyard excavated to search for dead babies in response to a bogus complaint filed by a local physician who believed homebirth was a criminal act akin to child abuse. Another midwife lost custody of her children in divorce proceedings because the opposing lawyer used her attendance at home deliveries to demonstrate social deviance and to paint her as an unfit mother. So much was at stake.

I began my talk, filing through slide after slide that demonstrated the midwives had achieved phenomenal outcomes—some of the best ever recorded for birth practitioners in any setting. More than 91 percent of the mothers in the Midwest practice who went into labor intending to deliver at home were successful. Only about 8 percent of homebirth attempts resulted in transport to the hospital. Six percent of the transports occurred during labor, less than 1 percent occurred in the early postpartum period for maternal complications, and less than 1 percent were a result of complications that affected the baby's health after delivery at home. In addition, only five infants were born with low birth weights (<2,500g), and only six infants were born slightly prematurely, between 34 and 36 weeks. I found no cases of life-threatening preterm delivery during the full 15 years of practice for this group of midwives! Rates of preterm and low birth weight infants for this practice are significantly lower than the average for the United States and for hospital deliveries. Midwives in this practice achieved these results despite serving a population that includes 30 percent low-income households and a disproportionate number of uninsured and underinsured mothers who are at higher risk for most complications including prematurity, low birth weight, and very low birth weight (Dominguez, 2008).

T A B L E 5.2   A Comparison of Material and Neonatal Outcomes for Women Who Began Labor Intending to Deliver at Home

Study and Geographic Location (n of Homebirths in the Study)	Labor before 37 weeks (n or %)		Maternal and Neonatal Transfers from Home to Hospital (n or %)			Spontaneous Vaginal Vertex Deliveries (%)		C-section (%)		Birth Weight < 2,500 g (n or %)		*Perinatal Mortality (n or rate per 1,000)	
	HB	CMP	IP	PP	Neo	HB	CMP	HB	CMP	HB	CMP	HB	CMP
Anderson & Murphy, 1995 USA n = 10,176	17	NA	8.2	0.8	1.0	ND	NA	0.3	NA	0.04	NA	4.2	NA
Murphy & Fullerton, 1998 USA n = 1,119	1.7	NA	8.3	0.8	1.1	99.6	NA	2.3	NA	n = 4	NA	2.5	Range: 1.3–2.1
Janssen et al., 2002 BC, Canada n = 862	ND	ND	16.5	ND	NA	90.4	68.4 (MD) 75.8 (MW)	6.4	18.2 (MD) 11.9 (MW)	0.8	2.0 (MD) 0.7 (MW)	n = 3	n = 2 (MD) n = 0 (MW)
Johnson & Daviss, 2005 USA and Canada n = 5,481	1.4	ND	10.1	1.3	0.7	ND	ND	3.7	Range: 19.0–24.0	1.1	2.4	2.0	1.7
Cheyney, Midwest Practice, ch. 5 n = 602	0.997	NA	6.75	0.67	0.84	97.8 (445/ 455)	NA	3.03 (18/ 595)	NA	1.15 (6/519)	NA	1.6	NA
Cheyney, Oregon Study, ch. 6 n = 362	0.0	ND	8.8	0.0	4.4	94.20	NA	5.52	NA	.83	NA	0.0/1?	NA

CMP = comparison group; HB = homebirth; IP = intrapartum transport in labor; PP = postpartum transport of mother; NEO = neonatal transport of infant after delivery at home; MD = medical doctor; MW = midwife; NA = not applicable; ND = no data.

*Data exclude neonates born with major congenital anomalies.

Ninety-seven percent of the women who went into labor intending to deliver at home delivered vaginally, producing a cesarean section rate of 3 percent for the total sample. First-time mothers had a cesarean section rate of about 9 percent, compared to a rate of 1 percent for mothers who had already had one baby successfully. The women who transported to the hospital for complications during labor had a midwife who stayed with them and advocated for as many low-tech options as possible. More than half of these women (54 percent) went on to deliver vaginally, while about 46 percent delivered by cesarean section. This result was interesting because many homebirth opponents assume that all or most home-to-hospital transports are emergencies. The fact that over half of the women who transported went on to labor and deliver vaginally indicates that this is not an accurate assumption.

The midwives were able to achieve impressive outcomes even though their sample included many higher risk births including breech deliveries, numerous vaginal births after a previous cesarean section, twins, and women delivering past their due dates. No maternal deaths occurred in the entire 15 years, and only one perinatal (the period immediately before and after birth) death occurred after an appropriate transport to the hospital. The perinatal mortality rate for this practice is 1.6/1,000 compared to 7/1,000 for the United States overall (WHO, 2007).

Midwives likewise achieved impressive results as measured by the health of newborns after birth. Apgar scores, as noted in Chapter 3, are the most common method of evaluating an infant's well-being; they are assigned in the hospital and at home at one and five minutes after delivery. A total score of 7–10 is considered to be normal, a score of 4–6 likely requires some resuscitation of the infant, and a score of 3 or lower requires immediate attention to prevent a catastrophe. In the Midwest sample, 473 records included information on Apgar scores; all but three infants in this subgroup had five-minute Agpar scores of seven or higher. The average five-minute Apgar score was 9.7 out of a possible high of 10, indicating that morbidity (the incidence of disease or other negative outcomes short of death) is extremely low in this sample. The total Midwest sample size of 602 is smaller than that of most other published studies on homebirth; however, the health outcomes from my study do not differ significantly from those reported in larger homebirth studies (see Table 5.2), suggesting that the Midwest sample size is large enough to produce reliable findings.

Furthermore, the Midwest sample provides the opportunity to explore questions about what constitutes "normal" mechanisms of delivery for humans. Consistent with the midwives' views, findings from the Midwest sample indicate that forward-facing infants, especially in first-time mothers, are problematic even for births occurring under the care of midwives. In the Midwest sample, I found 379 cases for which the position of the baby, mode of delivery (cesarean or vaginal), and the number of births for the mother are known. Of these 379 women, 369 delivered vaginally with infants in the following positions—93 percent backward facing, 5 percent forward facing, and 2 percent breech. None of the women who successfully delivered forward-facing babies vaginally were first-time mothers. This result suggests that midwives' impressions are correct; fetal position is less of a concern for women who have already delivered at least one infant.

The midwives are also correct in their impression that the frequency of transport to the hospital for medical intervention increases dramatically for forward-facing infants, especially in first-time mothers. The odds of transport for forward-facing presentations are 34 times greater than for backward-facing presentations. The most common reason for transport to the hospital for medical intervention is forward-facing presentation during labor, which explains 90 percent of all home-to-hospital transports. Again, this finding is important because the primary reason given by the medical establishment for opposing homebirth is that emergencies requiring transport might occur. I found only one emergency transport in 602 cases in the Midwest sample. The vast majority of transports were for labors that were progressing very slowly—the opposite of an emergency. Lucinda used to joke that the main problem precipitating a trip to the hospital was not that something bad was happening; it was that very little was happening!

Strong evidence supports midwives' experience-based impression that forward-facing infants result in higher rates of surgical delivery. The frequency of cesarean sections is indeed highest for first-time mothers with forward-facing presentations and lowest for mothers with at least one previous delivery and backward-facing presentations. Women laboring with forward-facing presentations are 813 times more likely to have a cesarean section than women with backward-facing presentations. Several clinical studies in hospital settings also demonstrate the connection between forward-facing infants in first-time mothers, prolonged labor, and increased likelihood of surgical delivery (Klein et al., 2001; Salmon & Drew, 1992; To & Li, 2000). The main difference between hospital studies and the Midwest homebirth sample is that the former result in cesarean section rates between 18 and 32 percent, while the latter is associated with a rate of only 3 percent. Homebirth midwives' views of normal birth and their strategies for safeguarding it are important keys to decreasing our nation's cesarean rate and associated rates of poor maternal and infant health outcomes.

As I neared the end of my presentation, an audience member stood and asked if she could interrupt. Louisa, a mother and doula who had participated in my study, said, "Can we stop for just a second and acknowledge Lucinda, Miriam, Carmen, Victoria, and the other homebirth midwives of this state? They are our freedom fighters. They put their families and their livelihoods at risk every day to honor a woman's right to choose where she gives birth. They stand up against an all-powerful medical system so that our babies can be born gently and peacefully at home, and I think we should stand up for them!" The room exploded in applause as the entire audience stood to honor the four midwives in the front row. It was the first time they had ever received public acknowledgment for their work. Their attempts to "fly under the radar" of their contentious medical model opponents has kept their identities hidden, preventing them from receiving the praise and recognition their clients feel they deserve. To mark the occasion, Lucinda proposed that we all go and get tattoos of trillium flowers. The roots of trillium flowers, also called "birthroot," were used historically to stop hemorrhages, but their use now is rare because the plant is endangered. I wear that tattoo today with my own gratitude for the women who not only helped me complete my doctoral research but also made me into a midwife.

THE OBSTETRIC DISCORDANCE HYPOTHESIS

I started this chapter with a discussion of evolutionary medicine, an approach in medical anthropology founded on the assumption that many contemporary health problems result from incompatibilities or discordances between the environments under which humans evolved and those that we live in today. The notion that these discontinuities produce disease, i.e., the discordance hypothesis, requires further reflection given what we now know about midwives' views of normal birth, their approaches to management, and their associated health outcomes.

Evolutionary reconstructions suggest that past birthing environments were substantially different from the ones experienced today, especially in urban and industrialized areas (Davis-Floyd & Cheyney, 2009). From an evolutionary medicine perspective, it is important to identify these differences because they often provide clues for reducing death and disease. By identifying differences or discordances between past and present birthing environments and behaviors, and by working to reduce these differences where appropriate, it may be possible to improve infant and maternal health. Homebirth midwives' approaches, when examined in the context of cross-cultural and evolutionary models of birthing across the primate order, are much more closely aligned with what evolutionary medicine would predict for human birthing patterns. In contrast, the way birth is performed and managed under current medical models tends to ignore and work against the evolved physiological and psychosocial needs of childbearing women. The overemphasis on impersonal, high-tech, and invasive medical procedures in human childbirth, in opposition to behavioral adaptations that are widespread in other primates and in all other pre-industrial cultures, result in poorer than expected outcomes in the United States.

The discordance hypothesis helps to explain why homebirth midwives are able to achieve such exceptional outcomes. My research suggests that homebirth midwives are applying the principles of evolutionary medicine, albeit inadvertently. Midwives' attempts to honor what they call "natural" models of birthing result in holistic models of care that more closely align with evolutionary, primate, and cross-cultural models of human birthing care. In essence, midwives decrease the degree of discordance between past and present birthing practices and behaviors. Approaches consistent with human biological and behavioral evolution include the following:

1. The presence of continual, usually female, support in labor, i.e. obligate midwifery.

2. Delivery in a place that feels safe and familiar to prevent or reduce the release of stress hormones that inhibit labor under dangerous conditions—remember the "white coat" and "weekend" effects discussed in chapter three.

3. Unencumbered movement during labor.

4. Upright pushing positions and squatting that increase the size of the birth canal.

5. The intake of easily digestible foods and fluids throughout labor, as opposed to the food restriction and fluid delivery through an IV that is the standard of care in hospitals.

6. The acknowledgement of a relatively wide range of normal for the duration of labor and pushing.

7. Holistic and intensive social support for mothers as they grow, birth and nurse their infants.

8. Time-honored, low-tech interventions for normalizing complicated labors.

The application of expensive and invasive, medical procedures that carry their own risks, have not improved, and in some cases have actually worsened, maternal and fetal outcomes in low-risk populations, though millions of dollars continue to flow unabated each year toward this end. Homebirth midwifery successes suggest that it is time to explore the possibility that less, and not more, technology combined with more holistic, time-intensive and evolutionarily sound care strategies can improve outcomes in the birthplace. High-tech approaches that are now the standard of care for all hospital deliveries in the United States should be reserved for the minority of births, such as the 8% of home-birthers in the Midwest sample who required hospital transport.

SUMMARY AND CONCLUSION

I conclude with a story that encapsulates the core question we have explored in this chapter: What is normal birth? Told by Lucinda, the story takes place at a gathering of midwives where they debated whether the perceived pain and difficulty of human birth is based in physical reality or whether it is simply a misogynistic, cultural construct. One midwife offered her controversial opinion: "I think that women experience birth as painful and difficult in this culture because they have been told all of their lives that that is how it is going to be. It is a self-fulfilling prophecy." Another midwife added: "Yes, you know I often think birth might just be like a bowel movement if the medical establishment didn't spend so much time telling women that it will be excruciating, and that they will need pain medications to get through it." Other midwives who seemed reluctant to speak up questioned this interpretation. One said: "Well maybe that has something to do with it, but I expected birth to be all rushes and highs and ecstasy because I had read *Spiritual Midwifery*,[1] and I was surprised to find that it still hurt like hell! It was nothing like a bowel movement." The debate raged and became heated until one highly experienced midwife, who was considered

---

1. *Spiritual Midwifery,* first published in 1977 by Ina May Gaskin, renames contractions "rushes" and describes unmedicated birth as orgasmic and ecstatic.

the "matriarch of the homebirth movement" in that community, finally spoke up. She ended the debate with one sentence that she felt encapsulated the key difference between births and bowel movements: "Shit doesn't breathe!"

Some midwives, medical anthropologists, and natural birth advocates who develop their perspectives in overt opposition to medical models of birth may be overcompensating as they explain away much or even all of the danger, pain, and difficulty attributed to human birth as simply a cultural construct, or as a political tool that ensures a monopoly on income-generating, "high-tech" hospital births. This culturally deterministic model of birth is no more accurate than an understanding of birth as inherently dangerous and routinely requiring massive biomedical intervention. As the midwife quoted above insinuated, birth may be a "natural," "normal" process in the life of most women, but it is not "normal" in the same way as other everyday bodily processes such as eating, sleeping, and excretion. More is always at stake during childbirth than in performing other "natural" biological functions. However, human childbirth does not need to be reconstructed as easy, painless, perfectly straightforward, or without pathological possibility to be understood as adaptive. Mechanisms of delivery can be complicated, prolonged, painful, difficult, and yet extraordinarily well adapted to the complex selective pressures resulting from the obstetrical dilemma. As Carmen said, "Birth is painful and challenging, but it is also almost always a safe and uncomplicated process for healthy and empowered women."

Although midwifery models of holistic, time-intensive, and preventative care are associated with positive clinical and psychosocial outcomes, their advocates are not above critique. Some academics and natural birth activists succumb to the naturalistic fallacy—the belief that what is natural is necessarily good. Just as technocratic models are based on the assumption that birth is dangerous, maladapted, and in need of medical interventions, so some alternative models may fail to acknowledge the complexity that results from the obstetrical dilemma. This complexity, however, does not mean that the widespread application of expensive technology in the birthplace is the only, or even the best, solution to the unique evolutionary compromises in pelvic shape and birth mechanisms faced by human mothers. Homebirth outcomes clearly indicate that alternative solutions are possible.

Mary Carlson of Harvard Medical School has coined the term "liberation biology" to describe the cooptation of biological research for use in gender politics (Angier 1999:xv). Moderated by feminist values and a revolutionary commitment to empower women, liberation biology, she believes, can heal the psychic wounds that come from living in a society that perceives the female (birthing) body as poorly adapted, dysfunctional, and inherently pathological. Midwives who attend normal, unmedicated homebirths every day gradually unlearn this "fact" of socialization and are left wondering why it is so difficult to accept that under most conditions birth is safe, women's bodies are well adapted to the challenges of reproduction, and that women are capable of caring for other women outside the institutional constraints of the hospital. If we are willing to listen, the voices and experiences of homebirth midwives will lead us to a (r)evolutionary obstetrics.

Chapter 6

Assessments of Safety and Risk
Bridging the Medical/ Midwifery Divide

Sitting in my office preparing a lecture, I receive a phone call. "Hello, my name is Dr. Jones. I'm a family practice physician in county X.[1] I understand you're a medical anthropologist specializing in homebirth, and I'm wondering if you would be willing to review a report we've written on causes of elevated perinatal[2] mortality in our county." I say that I would be happy to, open my email, and print the report. As I begin reading, my heart starts pounding, my face is flushed, and my red pen begins scribbling furiously across the page as if it has a mind of its own. The perinatal task force in this county has been investigating higher than expected rates of poor maternal and infant health outcomes and has decided that they can be explained by the prevalence of midwife-attended home deliveries in their county. What was their data source? Anecdotal, word-of-mouth stories that have circulated through local hospitals as nurses and doctors gossip about home-to-hospital transports—a phenomenon I call "birth story telephone" after the childhood game that demonstrates how

---

1. In this chapter, I use no names or pseudonyms for study participants and do not disclose the county. Given that the state's identity is known, participants requested that I use a minimum of identifiers to help protect their anonymity.

2. Remember from the last chapter that "perinatal" refers to the period immediately before and after birth.

facts change as stories pass through numerous tellers. The authors of the 30-page report have used this "evidence" to help explain their county's poor statistics and are wondering if I would be willing to contribute my expertise to help solve the "midwife problem" in their community. I would need a few margaritas before calling Dr. Jones back to discuss my feedback on the report!

My unique position as researcher and homebirth midwife has left me in an interesting position. I can see immediately how my expertise might help improve the scientific quality of this investigation. Specifically, I can help them to access and interpret actual sources of data in the form of Oregon vital records and interviews with the county's care providers. But how was I to respond without seeming hopelessly biased toward the midwifery cause? Many applied anthropologists who work with minority or marginalized cultural groups face this problem. How can we use our research findings and insider knowledge to act as advocates and cultural translators without having our expertise disregarded beneath claims of prejudice and partiality?

Some physicians and policymakers still believe that research can and should be completely value free, objective, and unbiased. Anthropologists have long discussed how researchers, as products of years of socialization in their culture, inevitably bring their own set of presuppositions to the table. These factors can never be removed fully from the research process. All research is subjective. The best we can do is to openly help readers of our work to understand our background and personal inclinations so they can turn the critical lens inward on our claims. Our methods may help to mitigate bias. We can be self-reflective and self-critical about our interpretations, and we can invite multiple, potentially conflicting, voices to be heard. We can, however, never make research truly value free.

I immediately set my thoughts to paper, developing a proposal for a more inclusive Community-Based Participatory Research Project designed to help evaluate the question of elevated mortality in this community. Such projects engage stakeholders at every stage of the research—from the formulation of research questions to data collection and analysis, and on to recommendations for policy or legislative change. In this way, study participants actually become a part of the process and not just subjects to be studied. In this chapter, I tell the story of the project that emerged, describing how we worked to include multiple voices, to produce a high-quality research product, and to translate findings into clear policy recommendations for use in addressing the glaring maternal-child health disparities that characterize this community. I have since served or consulted on several perinatal task forces across the nation, bringing the tools of anthological inquiry to bear on questions of how to safely integrate midwifery care into the maternal-child health system. Although at times infuriating, this task can also be exhilarating as we see our research move from the ivory tower of academia into new legislation and policies that have an immediate and substantial impact on mothers and babies.

FROM RESEARCH TO ADVOCACY

Several communities across the United States have elevated infant mortality rates and poor pregnancy outcomes, including higher-than-expected rates of prematurity and low birth weight in specific populations (Fischler, Kasehagen, Rosenberg, Nute Wiens, & Yusem, 2007). In many counties where perinatal mortality and morbidity markers exceed target goals, public health officials respond by appointing task forces charged with identifying the problem and proposing solutions. Comprised of researchers and clinicians, these task forces set out to identify factors, such as poverty or inadequate access to care, that correlate with suboptimal maternal-child health outcomes. Despite their good intentions, task forces are not always effective at improving health statuses for at-risk populations (Ahmed, Beck, Maurana, & Newton, 2004; O'Toole, Felix Aaron, Chin, Horowitz, & Tyson, 2003). The challenges of reconciling multiple and often conflicting perspectives, the variety of existing public health problems, the usual case of chronic underfunding, and low levels of engagement by some stakeholders (defined as groups invested in the solution) often prevent task forces from moving beyond rhetoric to evidence-based action (Felix & Stryer, 2003).

The Community-Based Participatory Research Project (Cargo & Mercer, 2008) that grew out of the initial phone call from Dr. Jones engaged community stakeholders in assessing the influence of midwife-attended home deliveries on their county's elevated rates of perinatal mortality and morbidity. Using a numbers and narratives approach, combining state vital records, local hospital information, and interviews with midwives and physicians, we uncovered several problems with homebirth safety tracking systems, as well as keys for improving relationships between home- and hospital-based practitioners. I begin with a discussion of what we found when we examined the safety of home deliveries, and then describe the sociopolitical context of midwife-physician interactions. I compare and contrast the perceptions of client risk level that sparked many of the conflicts between midwives and doctors and conclude with recommendations for facilitating mutual respect across competing models of care. My ultimate aim was to help the county and the state to improve access to safe, affordable, and culturally appropriate maternity care.

Our team set out to examine four research questions: (1) Are midwives contributing to the elevated mortality and morbidity rates documented in the research county? (2) If so, what is the difference in morbidity and mortality rates between licensed and unlicensed midwives? (3) Do women who begin labor intending to deliver at home have heightened risk, and could high-risk mothers who attempt to deliver at home be contributing to elevated mortality and morbidity rates? (4) Acknowledging that home delivery is a legal and an increasingly popular option in Oregon and across the nation, how can midwives and physicians better collaborate to ensure positive outcomes, both clinical and psychosocial, for families who choose birth at home with midwives?

INADEQUACIES OF VITAL RECORDS
AND MISSING INFORMATION

We started by obtaining permission from the Center for Health Statistics and the Offices of Disease Prevention and Epidemiology in Portland, Oregon, to study de-identified birth certificate records[3] for all deliveries occurring in the county during a six-year period. We imported the computer file and sorted 14,195 records by place of delivery using two preset categories: (1) private residence as place of delivery (330) and (2) other—a category that includes hospitals, clinics, physician offices, en route, birth on arrival, unknown, and other (13,865). Using statistical software, we calculated basic descriptive statistics for common indicators of maternal and infant health for all deliveries completed at home, including the birth weight of the infants, Apgar scores, and any complications or risk factors recorded on the birth certificates. In this phase of the study, we sought basic information on the frequency of births occurring at home in the county, the risk level of mothers completing home deliveries, and the health of infants born at home.

Our analysis indicated several areas where homebirth safety tracking in vital records was inadequate. The Oregon birth certificates we examined excluded several essential kinds of information required to adequately track homebirths. For example, they did not identify "planned home deliveries." In addition, the birth certificates captured only one of the three forms of home-to–hospital transports, identifying neonatal transports, but not postpartum or intrapartum transports. **Neonatal transports** occur when an infant successfully delivered at home is transferred to the hospital to treat complications immediately following the birth. **Postpartum transports** occur when a mother who successfully gives birth at home is transferred to the hospital, in most cases for bleeding that cannot be controlled by the anti-hemorrhagic medications available in a home setting. **Intrapartum transports** occur when a mother is transferred to the hospital because of complications that arise in labor before she delivers. Infants who are born in the hospital after an intrapartum transport were being erroneously lumped in with hospital births on the birth certificates.

In addition, we found that accidental and intentionally unassisted or "freebirth" deliveries (Griesemer, 1998; Wickham, 2008) were impossible to distinguish from intentional home deliveries attended by trained midwives. "Freebirthing" is a fast-growing movement in the United States and Europe where women attempt delivery at home without a trained attendant present. Most have the assistance of only

---

3. De-identified records have been cleansed of names and any other information that could be used to identify a particular individual.

their husband or partner. In this study we had no way to separate such unassisted births from planned, midwife-attended homebirths. In addition, we had difficulty acquiring records of intrapartum transports, those that occur during labor, from the local hospitals where midwives reported transferring clients. Only one of the three hospitals was able to produce detailed records for these transfers. As a result, we were limited in our calculations of overall rates of transport and in investigating mortality and morbidity in the transported subsample of intended home deliveries. The widely used definition of "home delivery" includes all births where the mother goes into labor intending to deliver at home, regardless of actual place of delivery (Fullerton et al., 2007). Monitoring homebirth safety requires keeping records of intended place of delivery and whether or not a trained attendant was present.

The low reliability and validity of birth certificate information (Northam & Knapp, 2006), along with the limitations in the Oregon tracking system described above, made it necessary for our project to add a second, qualitative phase that proved essential for helping to contextualize our statistical findings. We invited all homebirth midwives and hospital-based practitioners including obstetricians, certified nurse midwives, perinatologists—the obstetric specialists who care for women and fetuses with the highest levels of risk—and general practitioners who had attended deliveries in the county to participate in interviews about their experiences and perspectives on risk in childbirth and home-to-hospital transports.

We transcribed notes and audio-recorded interview texts into Word documents and analyzed them for commonly occurring themes. We then brought our analysis of themes and statistical findings back to communities in the county for comment during group interviews with midwives and at the county's taskforce meetings. We gave participants the opportunity to debate, critique, and verify our findings. And debate they did! As these initial presentations and our press releases started to attract publicity in the popular media, I began receiving hundreds of letters, emails, and voicemails both from advocates and detractors. During the next few months my research assistant and I assembled a sizeable collection of hate mail that called us everything from "pseudoscientists" to "baby murderers." Below I summarize our examination of the clinical outcomes from birth certificates and hospital records as well as the recurring themes from interviews that instigated these heated debates. I present them below in three sections: (1) tracking homebirth safety; (2) conflicting constructions of risk; and (3) providing care across the midwifery/medical divide. I conclude with a discussion of the specific recommendations for improved collaboration across a spectrum of maternity providers that emerged from this Community-Based Participatory Research Project.

TRACKING HOMEBIRTH SAFETY

Completed home deliveries (330) over the six-year study period accounted for 2.3 percent of all births occurring in the county. The neonatal transport rate calculated from birth certificates was 4.4 percent or 16 of 330. Information from the one hospital with records available showed that no mothers were transported for complications after successful home deliveries (postpartum transport rate of 0 percent), and that 32 intrapartum transports occurred, for an (under)estimated intrapartum transport rate of 8.8 percent. Even with missing data from two hospitals, these results indicate that intrapartum transports are the most common form of home-to-hospital transport, and that they are also the most likely to be lost in vital records tracking systems. For the laboring mothers taken to the one hospital, 37 percent went on to delivery vaginally, while 63 percent had a cesarean section. This translates into a cesarean section rate of about 6 percent, which is only one quarter of that reported for low-risk women undergoing planned hospital births (Janssen et al., 2002, 2009).

None of the infants born at home, including the 16 transported to the hospital for complications after birth, and none of the 32 who were born in the hospital after an intrapartum transport for which we have data, died during the neonatal period (defined as the first 28 days of life). Interviews indicate that one infant may have died after transfer during labor to one of the hospitals that does not track home-to-hospital transports, though we could not verify if this death occurred during the research period. As a result, we were unable to calculate a death rate for intended home delivery because we did not know the total number of intended homebirths, and because hospital records on intrapartum transport outcomes were incomplete. There were no perinatal deaths in the completed home delivery sample and no maternal deaths after attempted or completed home deliveries.

Thirty-eight percent of births completed at home were attended by licensed midwives, and 44 percent by unlicensed midwives. Naturopathic physicians, a certified nurse midwife, and medical doctors attended the remaining 18 percent. We found no significant differences in neonatal transport rates between licensed (8 of 128) and unlicensed (5 of 154) midwives. This finding, in particular, surprised physicians on the task force because they had expected unlicensed midwives to have higher rates of transports and poorer outcomes.

When we examined all midwife-attended home deliveries for low five-minute Apgar scores, where a score of six or below occurring five minutes after delivery is an indicator of neonatal illness. Only six of the 330 babies born at home had low five-minute Apgar scores. Ninety-eight percent of infants born at home had scores of seven or above, with a mean of 9.12 out of a possible 10—an indication of exceptionally good health in the babies born at home. In addition, no infants born in the hospital after an intrapartum transport had scores below seven, indicating a low level of illness even in those babies who mothers had significant enough complications during labor to require a transfer to the hospital. In comparing licensed vs. unlicensed midwives, we found no significant differences in rates of low five-minute Apgar scores (see Table 6.1). Again, these findings were surprising to some project participants.

Our results overall show that homebirth rates are too low and that birth outcomes at home are not sufficiently poor to be driving excess morbidity and mortality for the entire county. Moreover, unlicensed midwives do not produce worse birth outcomes than licensed midwives and, therefore, cannot be

T A B L E 6.1 **Apgar Score Comparison Between Unlicensed and Licensed Direct-entry Midwives**

	APGAR Score < 7 at 5 minutes %	APGAR Score ≥ 7 at 5 minutes %	x^2	Significance
Licensed Midwives	2.3 (N = 3)	97.7 (N = 128)	0.847	0.582 NO
Unlicensed Midwives	2.0 (N = 3)	98.0 (N = 150)		

the source of the county's problem. Unfortunately, we could not track the contribution of midwife-attended home deliveries, whether positive or negative, for some variables because of the limitations of vital records and hospital-based information systems. As alternative birth practices increase in popularity around the nation, we recommended that medical and public health offices across the United States conduct similar assessments of birth records to determine if all available birthing options can be adequately tracked for safety. In response to recommendations from this and other studies, Oregon adopted a new birth certificate in 2008 that includes identification of planned home delivery, making it possible to more accurately track the safety and frequency of home delivery.

CONFLICTING CONSTRUCTIONS OF RISK

Our third research question was, What is the extent of risk carried by women who go into labor intending to deliver at home? To answer this question, we attempted to create a risk index that would allow us to quantify the risk level of homebirth clients. Here we encountered a second major problem—we found remarkably little agreement between hospital-based practitioners and midwives on what constitutes a "high-risk" situation. We decided to create two separate risk indices, one developed from the perspective of the physicians on the task force and one agreed on by the midwives (see Appendix A).

The physicians' risk index identified 24 absolute, 15 non-absolute, and 25 additional risk criteria, where "absolute" refers to the indicator's nonnegotiable status and "non-absolute" allows for more flexible and individualized patient assessment (Lindauer, 2006). These absolute and non-absolute criteria derived from the Administrative Rules of the Oregon Board of Direct Entry Midwifery, a governor-appointed and Senate-confirmed advisory panel that sets guidelines for the practice of licensed midwifery in the state. I have served on this board since the beginning of 2008, allowing yet another opportunity to use my work in applied medical anthropology to help influence policy and practice. Oregon birth certificates contain information on 17 of the 24 absolute risk criteria, 12 of the 15 non-absolute risk criteria, and all 25 of the additional factors identified. According to the physicians' criteria extrapolated from birth certificates, 73 percent of all completed home deliveries in the county had at least one high-risk factor, and 26 percent had between two and four. According to this risk index, homebirth midwives have been attending a high percentage of high-risk births.

The midwives participating in this collaborative research project strongly opposed the list of additional risk criteria proposed by the physicians, claiming, for example, that women over 34 or under 18 years of age were not inherently higher risk. Oregon laws also do not prohibit breech, twins, or vaginal births after cesarean sections from being attended at home by midwives. Midwives view all of these conditions as often, but not always, higher risk, and they were opposed to including them in their risk index, opting instead for an index based on the absolute risk factors as set by the Oregon Board of Direct Entry Midwifery's Administrative Rules. When we evaluated the number of high-risk births occurring at home using the criteria agreed on by the midwives, the rate of "high-risk" births completed at home was only 4.4 percent. Clearly, midwives and physicians are not defining risk the same way! Should 73 percent (physicians' index) or 4.4 percent (midwives' index) of completed home deliveries be considered high-risk?

The answer to this question is important, given that the public health organizations that endorse homebirth as a safe and viable option—namely the World Health Organization and the American Public Health Association—do so with the caveat that only low-risk women are good candidates for home delivery. Investigators around the world have reported excellent outcomes for planned home deliveries for low-risk women, crediting skilled midwifery care with these results (de Jonge et al., 2009; Fullerton et al., 2007; Janssen et al., 2009), although screening procedures and formal guidelines for what constitutes a "low-risk client" are notably absent in the clinical and international maternal-child health literature.

Countries such as the Netherlands and New Zealand that have high rates of births at home and in birth centers (as high as 30 percent) have national guidelines for risk assessment and referral (DeVries, 2004). However, because these criteria are based on a well-organized system for the transfer of care across birth settings, they are not clearly applicable to the Unites States. Midwives in the above countries practice in cultures where homebirth is common and the obstetric system is well-integrated with efficient information-sharing between home, hospital, and birth-center settings. These countries recognize their responsibility to maintain homebirth as a safe and viable option. Until such a climate prevails in the United States, homebirth midwives must devise their own guidelines for risk assessment and client screening with reference to state or regional standards, the quality and availability of medical backup, practitioner experience level, and legal constraints (Vedam and Kolodji 1995). The system in the United States inevitably breeds enormous variation in risk criteria and standards of care, not only between midwives and obstetricians as this study has identified but also within groups of midwives. During transports, these disparate paradigms of birth and risk come together, forcing midwives and physicians to find ways to communicate and care for families across cultural and philosophical divides. My experiences working with midwives and physicians suggest that their cooperation is not always successful.

SPEAKING ACROSS THE MIDWIFERY/ MEDICAL DIVIDE

Our open-ended interviews and group discussions elicited in-depth, qualitative information on risk perception and the political and ethnographic contexts of interactions between home- and hospital-based providers (see Photo 6.1). Themes that emerged both from midwives and physicians focused almost exclusively on the disputed terrain of home-to-hospital transport. The cultural opposites of home and hospital care often generate emotionally charged opinions on both sides, and the themes that emerged from care providers' narratives indicate deeply conflicting perceptions of risk, as well as conflicts between larger models of birthing care that inform designations of risk.

Interviews with hospital-based providers revealed three key themes that differed substantially from those found in midwives' narratives: (1) the belief that home delivery is substantially more dangerous than current studies suggest; (2) the fear and frustration generated when physicians must assume the risk of caring for another provider's transported patient; and (3) the belief that midwives make high-risk situations more dangerous by being difficult to work with due to poor charting[4] and their defensive, antagonistic personalities.

Home Delivery as Dangerous

The first theme—the belief that home delivery is more dangerous than studies indicate—was widely shared by hospital-based practitioners who participated in our interviews. With only one exception, they expressed the view that birth

PHOTO 6.1 Author and research assistant, Courtney Everson, conducting an interview with a midwife (photograph by Elaine Taylor).

---

4. Both midwives and physicians keep track of the details of clients' care and health history through a process called charting. These charts become part of clients' medical records, and they are consulted frequently during the provision of care.

must occur in the hospital to be safe. One physician stated that low-risk women should be able to choose a home delivery with a well-trained midwife, but he was careful to stress his concern that midwives in his locality might be caring for too many high-risk patients: "My point is not so much that high-risk women can't ever have homebirths, but I'm concerned that midwives might not be giving the appropriate extra care." He believed that the mismanagement of high-risk patients by midwives fuels discord between midwives and doctors and makes hospital practitioners skeptical of the published studies on home delivery. He said of his colleagues, "When they hear that homebirth is relatively safe, they just don't believe it because they all know of cases where a mother or baby has transported and they were in danger. The findings just don't fit with their experiences." While all of the hospital providers who participated in interviews and in the task-force presentation of preliminary findings agreed that the vast majority of home-to-hospital transports were not emergencies, they remained deeply influenced and angered by the few emergencies they had experienced. Being forced to take over these cases, or even thinking about having to do so, produced a fear and animosity not easily assuaged, even by a positive outcome.

Another physician discussed his belief that midwives assist too many high-risk women at home: "How can obstetricians be expected to be nice and respectful to homebirth midwives when they are forced to clean up their messes, when they have to take care of a mother and the baby dies?" Even when deaths do not occur and the ultimate outcomes are positive, concerns are still evident. One hospital-based nurse midwife asserted, "It is true that few transports are emergencies, but what really frustrates me is what I would call mismanagement. You know, the water has been broken for three days or she's been dilated to six centimeters for 12 hours. That's not an emergency, but it's also not good care! Why gamble with high-risk situations?" Echoing the concerns of her colleague, she continued: "It is just impossible for us to believe that homebirth is safe because we have seen all the times when it has not been. It makes us skeptical of the literature. We're living it, and we don't see it as safe."

Fear and the Transfer of Risk

The second theme—fear of accepting a transported patient with a serious or life-threatening complication and the burden of risk this transfers to the physician—emerged in all hospital practitioner interviews and in discussions with perinatal task-force members. Physicians expressed concern over "preventable deaths" in high-risk homebirth patients and bemoaned the burden placed on them when midwives transport what they called "train wreck" births. One obstetrician said, "I'm getting older, and I can't retire because I'm worried about these home-born babies. Who is going to be there to help these babies?" Another physician explained, "Imagine our perspective. This woman comes in with her midwife after a failed homebirth. We're out in the hall arguing about who is going to go in there. There is a lot of risk involved for us, plus we know we are likely to have a hostile interaction or a noncompliant patient. It's not something we're going to look forward to."

All homebirth midwives who participated in our interviews cited this problem as well, and they offered empathy for physicians. One said, "During a transport, you can tell they [the doctors] are really fearful, they're afraid because no one knows what's going on, and they always have litigation hanging over their heads like a dark cloud.... There isn't any mal-intent. They are just so out of their comfort zones and they're scared that homebirthers are going to refuse procedures because they're so pro–natural birth." Another midwife explained: "We wouldn't want that either—to have to care for someone we've never met who may or may not be in crisis, knowing the family doesn't want to be there [the hospital]." Both sides openly recognize that transports place midwives and physicians in vulnerable positions precisely when working together and communicating across their differences is essential to producing positive outcomes. However, they could not come to agreement on how to rectify the problem.

The Difficulty of Working with Midwives

Doctors and nurses discussed a third concern about midwives—poor charting and difficult personalities. All hospital-based participants emphasized the difficulty they had working with some homebirth midwives, citing confusing or poor charting that includes "a whole bunch of psychosocial stuff that we don't care about, like her diet in the first trimester or how the women in her family have given birth." Another physician said, "Everyone uses different charts and we're getting so used to electronic charting now, you can't find anything that makes sense to you, and meanwhile this mother and baby need help. It's frustrating." Add to this that physicians find some midwives to be "difficult," "defensive," and "antagonistic," and it is not surprising that many hospital providers are anxious about assisting with homebirth transports. When midwives advocate certain treatment options for their clients, physicians report feeling "put on the defensive" and "attacked." One doctor explained: "They come in for our help and then they act like they are trying to protect the patient from us. That is insulting! We're there to help, and they act like we're out to section [OB-speak for cesarean section] every woman just to make our lives easier."

When asked if they had ever participated in a positive home-to-hospital transport, all of the hospital providers admitted that most are positive and that many midwives are good at charting and communication. They expressed appreciation for some who did an excellent job of preparing their patients for the hospital, which helps to "make mothers more compliant." Nonetheless, they are heavily influenced by their experiences with homebirth midwives that they perceived as hostile. Unless specifically prompted, they are significantly more likely to discuss negative experiences.

In contrast, midwives asserted that most of their interactions with doctors and nurses were friendly and supportive, even citing instances where physicians allowed them to continue to participate in a client's care after transport. All of them also told stories of "difficult," "bad," or "humiliating" transports, where physicians insulted or mocked them in front of their clients. Nonetheless, midwives were much more likely to emphasize the collaborative model of care they strive for and sometimes achieve. Their attitudes may be borne of necessity; while most obstetricians can envision a system without homebirth midwives, midwives cannot provide safe, effective care without a reliable system of medical backup.

Midwives' discussions of risk assessment and transport revolved around three key themes, reflecting views that differ substantially from those of hospital doctors and nurses. These include (1) the defense of holistic and co-negotiated assessments of risk; (2) physicians' tendency to judge homebirth midwives by "the exception, rather than the rule"; and (3) the failure of physicians to take responsibility for their roles in contributing to poor maternal-child health outcomes.

Holistic Perceptions of Risk

The first theme—the defense of holistic and co-negotiated assessments of risk—was discussed by every homebirth midwife as one of the core values of the midwifery model of care. One midwife said, "The midwifery model of care is about acknowledging more than just clinical risk. It's about the whole person.... There are other kinds of risk. There is psychosocial risk, the risk of unnecessary procedures, the risk of having to parent from a position of victimization and regret. Does that matter? I think it should." Midwives also discussed how differences among the clientele they serve necessitate co–decision making. One said, "You know homebirthers. They are not typically people who are just told what to do. They are people who wear shirts that say 'Birth: Have it your way.'... They want information so they can filter that information through their own values and needs and come up with their own decisions. We don't have full power over them." The midwives were careful to stress that they were not placing blame on high-risk women who choose to give birth at home, and they emphasized that the responsibility to ensure safety is ultimately shared by both mother and midwife. One midwife said, "As the experts, we can't just say, 'Well, she [the mom] chose this,' and wash our hands of it. We are involved in the decision-making process, and we have to own up to our part in it. It's just that the power of choice is truly shared in our model."

All midwives stated that the vast majority of their clients are low-risk and deeply committed to their babies' health. As one midwife explained, "Homebirthers don't love their babies any less than hospital birthers." Midwives also pointed out that, due to selection bias, they see more women who have "issues with the hospital." They believe that homebirth clientele draw the "risk line in the sand" in different places because of their unique values, life contexts, and personal histories. One midwife explained:

> Take someone who feels like her first cesarean was unnecessary, and she had a tough postpartum period as a result, can you see how she might push staying at home longer than someone who feels like going to the hospital is really no big deal? I can give them information, but I can't always decide what is best for them. At most, I can decline to offer them care if it goes too far outside my comfort zone, but you

have to know too that a small percentage of these women will just go and do an unassisted birth then. It's a hard line to draw, because I'm not the only one involved.

Another midwife, discussing the same theme, said the following:

It makes me really mad when you end up transporting someone who is higher risk and the doctor is giving you this nasty look and yelling at you in the hall and acting like it's your ignorance that has brought this on. I mean do they just do whatever they want to with their mothers? Don't they have to get consent too? I always say: "Listen, you know how you have people who want an elective c-section, and it's a small percentage, like 2–3 percent, but you have them, and they are really set against having a vaginal birth? Well we're dealing with the opposite end of the spectrum. So, try to understand. We are serving moms who are hoping to avoid much of what you have to offer, and that means I am serving a really different clientele. It's not fair for you to judge me by your hospital's standards of care and not by the midwifery model that guides my work.

Judged by the Exception, Not the Rule

Midwives also discussed a second and related theme of feeling judged "by the exception and not the rule," which they assert leads to deep misunderstandings between homebirth midwives and their medical colleagues. In addition to feeling blamed for the infrequent, higher-risk client, midwives expressed frustration with physicians for doubting or simply not knowing about the literature on home delivery's safety. One said, "Doctors don't know about the CPM 2000 study,[5] which had a sample size of almost 6,000 and showed that mortality was low even when breech and twins were included in the sample. What they see is our transports, and then out of that, they seem to only remember the more critical ones. They have no idea how many births we do that go beautifully at home because they, of course, never see those." Another midwife said, "From their perspective, every homebirth is a transport, otherwise how would they know about it? So they are thinking about our transfer rate or even our mortality rate, but they don't have any idea what the denominator is." She continued: "We have these big scientific studies that show we are safe, but docs can't believe them. Why? Because they don't fit with their experiences. So here we are at a total impasse."

This sense that they are being judged by the exception and not the rule is an important point, given the difficulty of tracking homebirth outcomes through vital records as uncovered in the first part of our project. This limitation allows physicians to form opinions on the safety, and thus the acceptability, of home delivery based on anecdotal data and perception, rather than on scientific

---

5. This is a reference to Johnson and Daviss (2005).

evidence gathered in their communities. One midwife called this way of thinking "medicine-based evidence, instead of evidence-based medicine."

Furthermore, midwives often engage in the same process of internalizing highly biased information on hospital births. Because homebirth midwives develop their perceptions of hospital staff and practices during defensive and, occasionally, openly hostile transport situations, as well as through clients who come to them after "traumatic hospital births," many of their views are equally prejudiced. This double-sided bias further fuels the discord that can develop between medical and midwifery models of care and between home- and hospital-based providers. Any potential overlap in values or practices tends to be overlooked, thus reinforcing the midwifery/obstetric divide and an "us vs. them" mentality that appears difficult, if not impossible in some cases, to bridge.

Taking Responsibility for Poor Outcomes

The third theme—the belief that physicians fail to take responsibility for their roles in poor maternal-child health outcomes—stems from the frustration inherent in the first two themes. Homebirth midwives resent the negative focus and perception of blame "laid at our feet by the medical establishment." One midwife, in critiquing physicians who oppose homebirth, said:

> We do 1 percent of all births in this country; 99 percent occur in the hospital, and 90 percent are physician-attended. So hospitals are doing the vast majority of the births in this country, and where does the U.S. rank in terms of maternal and infant health? Are we the best? No. We are toward the bottom. We have some of the worst outcomes in the developed world. When are they going to own up to that and start saying "what can we do to make birth safer and to improve access to care for mothers and babies?" instead of saying, "let's try to get rid of homebirth altogether."

Another homebirth midwife tied this argument to rates of preterm birth: "I don't like being treated as the enemy, like women need to be protected from us, like we are forcing them to give birth at home. My phone is ringing off the hook with women looking for another option. Homebirth is not killing babies.... Preterm birth is! If doctors want to save babies, they need to figure out how to reduce prematurity." Another midwife added, "We do 1 percent of births, with a mortality rate of 2–3/1000. That is not a lot of babies. Over 35 percent of infant deaths in this country are related to complications of preterm. Prematurity is by far the largest killer of babies. I mean, why is the American Medical Association after us and not focusing on the real issues?" This comment is in response to the American Medical Association's House of Delegates' *Resolution 205 on Home Deliveries* (American Medical Association, 2008) which calls for federal legislation to establish hospitals and hospital-based birth centers as the only safe delivery options. The homebirth midwives who participated in this project described Resolution 205 as self-serving and, along with some of the more subtle forms of discrimination they face during transports, one of the many ways legitimate discussions on how to best meet the clinical and psychosocial needs of childbearing women in the United States are silenced.

Clashes of worldviews and value systems related to birth contribute to the fractured working relationships reported by participants in this and other studies on home-to-hospital transports (Davis-Floyd, 2003, 2004; Johnson & Davis-Floyd, 2006). Physicians discussed clear concerns over the safety of home-birth and reluctance to assist with transports, while midwives cited tension and a lack of respect for their model of care as the primary reasons why they do not "feel safe" or "welcome to participate" in the perinatal task-force meetings in their community, despite repeated attempts by public health officials to involve them over the years. The social and political contexts of midwifery and obstetric interactions make our fourth and final research question, in some ways, the most difficult to answer. Acknowledging that home delivery is a legal and popular option in many states, how can midwives and physicians work together to ensure positive outcomes for families who choose to birth at home with midwives?

RECOMMENDATIONS AND THE NEED
FOR POLICY CHANGE

Compulsory interactions that occur during transports bring biomedicine's ascendant knowledge system into contact with the devalued and marginalized knowledge system of homebirth midwifery. This contact can function either to entrench and solidify divisions or to begin healing the gap. Robbie Davis-Floyd (2003) describes three possible outcomes of interactions during home-to-hospital transports that she terms disarticulation, fractured articulation, and smooth articulation. **Disarticulation** occurs when there is no overlap in or correspondence of information between the midwife and the hospital staff. **Fractured articulation** of knowledge systems results from partial or incomplete correspondence of perspectives, and **smooth articulation** results when the interactions between midwife and medical personnel involve mutual accommodation or the respectful sharing of knowledge and power (Davis-Floyd, 2003). Our project participants offered four suggestions for decreasing fractured and disarticulated interactions and increasing smooth articulations; two came from midwives, and two came from hospital-based practitioners.

First, midwives requested that the hospital staff show respect for them during transports and in dialogues over the best course of treatment. Midwives have access to intimate knowledge about the mother, her pregnancy, and her labor, that is essential to the diagnosis and treatment plan. Respectful communication increases the likelihood that this information can be shared and used beneficially. As the transported woman finds herself in a new and unfamiliar environment facing unknown interventions, she inevitably looks to her midwife for support and guidance. Any perceived devaluing of the midwife by hospital personnel can be internalized as a criticism of the mother's choice to attempt a home delivery. This means that no matter how supportive the staff is of the patient, if they are dismissive, judgmental, or condescending toward the midwife, the mother may feel alienated. Conversely, collegial interactions with the midwife communicate respect for the mother's autonomy and right to choose place of delivery. Any doubts about the midwife or expressions of frustration, explicit or implied, should not occur in the family's presence.

Second, midwives cautioned hospital staff against assuming that someone who has attempted a home delivery will necessarily decline hospital procedures. Homebirth clientele run the gamut from families who decline all prenatal testing, including routine ultrasounds, to those who request every biomedical test available. For most women who prefer to give birth at home, the decision to transport amounts to a tacit acknowledgment of the need for interventions available only in the hospital. Midwives suggest that physicians give an honest assessment, avoid scare tactics, and offer their recommendations in a collaborative manner. Physicians should recognize that homebirth clients are likely to ask numerous questions and want extensive explanations. This behavior does not mean they intend to decline a procedure. As discussed in previous chapters, homebirth clients have internalized a model of care that involves detailed discussion of options, a focus on informed consent, and valuing of client input.

Hospital practitioners offered a third recommendation, emphasizing the need for "timely transport with clear charting," along with a desire to assist with "complications, not crises." Acknowledging that rare and unforeseen emergencies can occur, physicians request that midwives make it a priority to allow adequate time to talk prior to meeting the patient and assuming responsibility for care. Calm, informative discussion that familiarizes the doctor with the complications leading to transport, along with the need to read through the patient's chart, all require substantial time. Homebirth midwives are encouraged to keep this in mind and to discuss this with their clients prior to a transport. Project participants also suggested that a standard transport form be developed that includes all of the key information that hospitals require to make their initial assessments. A standard form developed out of this project is now being tested in several Oregon communities. In addition, if midwives and physicians can confer over a case, and then enter the room together with a plan to discuss with the client, they are likely to convey a sense of collaboration and camaraderie between midwife and physician to the mother. This can, in turn, reduce her fear of being judged and further facilitate smooth articulations and mutual accommodation.

The fourth and final recommendation comes from physicians who requested that midwives make a greater effort to prepare all clients for the possibility of transport, with the expressed intent of demystifying and devilifying interventions such as epidural pain relief, pitocin augmentation, and cesarean section. Many homebirthers elect to deliver outside of the hospital precisely because they wish to avoid these procedures, seeing them as overused and riskier than a "natural" vaginal delivery. Clients must be able to transition from a critique of interventions to understanding them as necessary in some high-risk situations when attempts at an unmedicated home delivery have not been successful. Accepting medical intervention can be especially difficult for women who have spent their pregnancies defending the decision to deliver at home. Preparing clients for potential transport is essential to smooth articulations.

Collectively, our findings from vital records and provider narratives facilitated the development of applied recommendations, as well as specific protocols designed to help obstetricians and midwives stem the home/hospital divide. In Appendix B you can read one of the policies that resulted from this study that I coauthored with an obstetrician colleague. We are currently pilot-testing this protocol in several communities.

SUMMARY AND CONCLUSION

In conclusion, this Community-Based Participatory Research Project identified areas where state and county perinatal task forces can improve tracking of alternative birth practices. We also made recommendations for changes to birth certificates that will assist communities in monitoring homebirth safety, allowing them to capture intended place of delivery and whether a trained attendant was present for the birth. Our project also increased dialogue, leading participants to acknowledge that perinatal task-force discussions and interventions do not occur in a cultural vacuum. The ethnographic contexts and relationships between community power brokers involved in addressing public health dilemmas must be made explicit. The use of a community-based, participatory approach was particularly useful in this project because it led to the inclusion of previously excluded voices. Narratives collected across a spectrum of care providers in both home and hospital birth settings provided a deeper understanding of different perceptions of childbearing risk, while also clearly delineating areas for improving communication across the home/hospital divide. The coalescence between qualitative and quantitative findings ultimately provided a nuanced account of homebirth outcomes, allowing us to move beyond a simplistic reporting of perinatal health statistics. Finally, our approach enabled us to be cognizant and inclusive of local political realties, resources, and worldviews that inform choices around birthing options.

We concluded this particular project with the sense that articulations between providers were more fractured than smooth, though we remain hopeful that we may eventually achieve mutual accommodation and cooperation. In some communities, physicians and midwives are beginning to view transports and task-force meetings as opportunities for collaboration and the development of cultural sensitivity around differing values, perspectives, and experiences. Medical anthropologists have important applied roles to play as cultural brokers, helping to span multiple markers of difference. Working with providers across the spectrum, we can achieve comprehensive, supportive, and effective maternity care that facilitates smooth, rather than fractured, articulations.

Chapter 7

Hope for Mothers
and Babies

Throughout this book, embedded in the unfolding story of my field research and experiences attending home deliveries, I have explored the models, practices, and health outcomes associated with homebirth midwifery care in the United States while raising questions about the effectiveness of high-tech obstetrics. In Chapter 1, I reviewed the history of birth's movement from home to hospital and the associated decline in midwifery as a respected profession in the United States. I reported the most recent figures on maternal and infant health in global perspective and laid the economic and political groundwork for understanding the current marginalization of homebirth midwives. The position midwives hold today at the fringes of what is considered acceptable or responsible birthing behavior powerfully influences the politico-legal environments where they practice, as well as the degree to which their voices are either heard or silenced in maternity care reform discussions. It is my hope that a better understanding of the history of homebirth midwifery and the politics of for-profit medicine will lead to a multi-sided dialogue around how to address the central problem facing the U.S. maternity care system today—the pattern of increasing costs, poorer than expected outcomes, and rising disparities in access to care for poor, rural, and uninsured or underinsured women and babies.

In Chapter 2, I reviewed the anthropological literature on birthing models, critiquing the dualism set up by previous scholars between midwifery/holistic and medical/technocratic models of childbirth. I examined the components of each of these models and then, using the experiences and stories collected through extensive interviews and participant-observation, I discussed the flexibility and movement that actually exist within what has been called too simplistically the midwifery model of care. Models or views of birth vary according to several factors, including the midwife's experience level, the risk category of particular mothers, barriers to practice, physician backup, issues of legality, and the midwife's own birth experiences. In reflecting on what ways of seeing birth might mean in practice for midwives' clients, I proposed that variation and flexibility within midwifery models of care may be better matched to the biocultural variability of unmedicated human birth produced by the five Ps of labor (*passageway, powers, passenger, psyche*, and *position*). This compatibility between midwifery approaches and the biology of birth may partially explain the excellent outcomes associated with home delivery.

In Chapter 3, I discussed homebirth practices as simultaneously ritual performance and evidence-based medicine. I examined midwifery protocols and standards of care through the lens of symbolic anthropology, analyzed birth at home as an alternative rite of passage, and discussed how rituals can become biologically embedded through a process called "somaticization" that powerfully connects the mind and body. Midwives and their clientele reject notions of their bodies as inferior or as necessarily in need of major medical intervention during the childbearing process. They also redefine technology as a choice of last resort that is largely ancillary to the innate wisdom and sufficiency of the unmedicated birthing body. For many women, birth at home is a political act of resistance, enabling them to reject mainstream values inherent in technological models of birth; they actively create, live, and embody a more intimate way of giving birth.

In Chapter 4, I examined mothers' birthing narratives in an attempt to explain how women decide to deliver at home in a society that does not see this choice as safe or responsible. Women's stories of homebirth allow us to see how they manage fears associated with the "just in case something bad happens" argument that provides the main rationale for hospital birth. By challenging established forms of authoritative knowledge, by valuing alternative and more embodied ways of knowing, and by cultivating intimacy in the birthplace, homebirthers justify the decision to birth at home.

In Chapter 5, I discussed midwives' views of normal birth, the practices they use to help ensure "that births stay normal," and the clinical consequences of these approaches as measured by their associated outcomes. Homebirth midwives' experiences and the combined health outcomes from their practices have much to add to academic debates over what constitutes "normal birth" for humans. Although little evidence exists to support the unqualified "all mechanisms of labor are normal" perspective, my findings do suggest areas where current medical parameters of normal could be expanded. Midwives' focus on prevention over intervention, the acknowledgment of a wider range of normal for labor's duration, and time-honored, low-tech techniques for optimal fetal positioning are associated with significantly lower rates of medical intervention and surgical delivery. The debate over normal birth may lead to a better understanding of when to intervene in birth and when to simply support women to do what their bodies have evolved to do. Homebirth practices and outcomes suggest clear directions for the reform of expensive, "high-tech" interventions that have not resulted in the hoped for improvements in maternal and infant health.

In Chapter 6, I told the story of my work on an Oregon county task force charged with the job of evaluating homebirth midwifery's contribution to the poor birth outcomes documented in their community. Results overall showed that homebirth rates are too low and birth outcomes at home are not sufficiently poor to be driving excess morbidity and mortality for the entire county. Moreover, unlicensed midwives do not produce worse birth outcomes than licensed midwives and, thus, are not the source of the county's problem. Open-ended interviews and focus group discussions elicited in-depth, qualitative information on risk perception, indicating that the cultural opposites of home and hospital care often generate emotionally charged opinions on both sides. A better understanding of conflicting opinions allowed my co-researchers and me to make recommendations for smoother articulations between homebirth midwives and hospital-based nurses and doctors. Chapter 6 provides an example of how medical anthropology can move from research to advocacy and policy change with the exciting potential to positively affect the lives of our study participants.

These chapters paint a picture of homebirth midwifery that has much to offer policy and practice in the applied realm of public health, as well as in more theoretically oriented fields of medical anthropology. In particular, my research and experiences with homebirth midwives call into question the political and economic motivations for the current marginalization and, in some states, the criminalization of direct-entry midwifery. All available evidence suggests that for low-risk women who engage in prenatal care with a qualified midwife, and have access to medical backup when a complication arises, that homebirth is an empowering, low-cost, safe, and viable birthing option. Currently no evidence-based justification exists for the American College of Obstetrics and Gynecology's oppositional stance on home delivery. The safety and efficacy of less technological, more holistic, individualized, and time-intensive approaches used in midwifery models of care are good evidence-based medicine, which, unfortunately, is the antithesis of what most Americans believe. By getting to know the midwives and mothers who advocate for a woman's right to choose a home delivery, we can begin to understand alternative viewpoints and, as a result, think more critically about the culturally constructed assumptions and financial motivations that structure birthing options in the United States today.

My fieldwork and experiences as a midwife vividly illustrate that the reporting and interpretation of biocultural research, and especially reporting and interpretation related to birth outcomes, are unavoidably political acts. Discussions of birthing models, homebirth rituals, and midwives' perspectives on how to define and support normal birth are not just theoretical abstractions; they have both clinical and economic consequences for real people. The anthropology of praxis requires that researchers not only examine the complexities of human biologies and cultural systems, but that we also take responsibility for the political consequences of our research. In the next section, I explain the final and most recent outcome of my work with homebirth midwives—my role as expert witness in federal and state-level legislative hearings where I am being called with increasing frequency to testify on the culture and safety of homebirth midwifery.

MEDICAL ANTHROPOLOGY AT THE STATE HOUSE

My research combined with my position on the Oregon Board of Direct Entry Midwifery has lead to many opportunities to testify in legislative hearings— something I was initially a little nervous to do. My doctoral training did not prepare me for how to talk to the media or give me the opportunity to see research moved into the realm of writing legislation and lobbying. Over the last few years, as I have gained experience testifying, I have become more confident and passionate about it, and now I see the opportunity to address legislators as one of the most exciting parts of being an applied medical anthropologist. I have been heckled and booed, and I have served as the impetus for many a stormy departure from a presentation. But, I have also received hundreds of thank-yous from midwives, mothers, and physicians around the country who express hope that my work will at least open a dialogue. Varied responses to my research have taught me that cultural norms have an incredible power to determine what we see and what we miss. The assumption that birth is dangerous and requires extensive medical management has blinded us to other possibilities; removing these cultural blinders is a major task.

In 2007, my doctoral work came full circle when a state near where I apprenticed called me back to testify in state House hearings. Legislators asked me to comment on the cultural context and public safety benefits of legalizing direct-entry midwifery. The writers of the bill hoped my testimony would persuade important fence-sitting representatives to vote to make birth at home with a state-licensed, direct-entry midwife a legally protected option. The night before the hearings we met with representatives sponsoring the legislation, brainstorming strategies to preempt anticipated arguments against the bill. We worked late into the night strategizing and finalizing my PowerPoint presentation. In the morning, we entered the hearing chamber and were met with a sea of television cameras and a packed audience; the opposition had filled the room with our detractors. A handful of homebirth mothers, babies, and midwives, who were putting themselves on public record and endangering their abilities to practice, were also present. I was the first of three experts to testify. Our instructions were to hold all questions and comments until the end of the last presentation.

I approached the podium and began a presentation with the most recent figures on infant and maternal mortality in the United States generally and in their state more specifically. The numbers clearly called attention to the problems associated with the current, legal system of technological birthing care. Background chatter, snickering, and overt heckling from the physicians in the audience started on the second slide. Speaking over the hostile noises, I went on to explain the key reasons why women choose a homebirth, followed by the most recent research on safety and cost savings. I concluded with a critique of the current legal status of midwifery in their state, where it is legal for a woman to deliver at home alone but not in the presence of a trained, direct-entry midwife. Mothers may legally deliver unassisted or attended by their husbands, friends, or a member of their church. Homebirth care only becomes a felony when a woman hires a midwife who is trained to attend home deliveries. In this case, authorities can prosecute the midwife for practicing medicine without a license.

This Midwestern state has one of the largest populations of pregnant, uninsured, and underserved women in the United States. Many women in rural areas must drive from one to two hours to reach the closest obstetrician. State licensing of direct-entry midwives is an ideal solution to this crisis of access, as well as to the poor outcomes and rising health disparities between high- and low-income families that plague this state. Members of the House health care committee seemed to be listening, albeit with great difficulty thanks to the disruptive opposition.

After my colleagues had made their presentations, the floor opened for questions. The "questions" came in the form of challenges and personal attacks, to which the three of us did our best to respond. Several physicians shared birthing horror stories where mothers and babies died catastrophic deaths, or came close to doing so, in the hospital. At first, I could not figure out how emphasizing the frequency of death and poor outcomes in the hospital could possibly be helping them prove their point—that homebirth should remain outlawed. I was compelled to point out that these stories were anecdotal and that, in general, we do not want to write laws or develop policies based on anecdotal evidence. How is evidence of death in the hospital relevant to questions about the legality of homebirth care? Partway through I realized that the intent of these stories was to establish that birth is dangerous with the subtext or implication that even when everything is done correctly, i.e., the birth occurs in the hospital, attended by highly trained surgical specialists with access to state-of-the-art medical interventions, babies still die. Homebirth seems absurd and reckless in this light. Because it is so difficult to check this socially engrained supposition at the door of a legislative hearing, the birth horror story strategy is incredibly effective, even in a room full of self-proclaimed scientists. I was glad to have learned this lesson early and in my presentations and responses have made sure to punctuate research findings with my own powerful anecdotes.

One obstetrician who was particularly angry with me during this hearing made the argument that "the data on home and hospital birth outcomes was like comparing apples and oranges." The hospital has a large percentage of higher risk births and because homebirth families are self-selected and lower risk, "of course midwives will have better outcomes." I countered that although some of the early studies from the 1980s failed to control for risk level of the mother, several recent studies have demonstrated comparatively poorer outcomes for hospital births even when only low-risk women are included in the analysis (Janssen et al., 2002, 2009). I added that midwives are only asking for the right to attend low-risk women at home and, by his own admission, "of course midwives will have better outcomes." Snickers and cheers arose from the midwives and some of the members of the health care committee.

Initially, I was taken aback and even distraught over the strength of the animosity and seething hatred I felt at this and other hearings. My physician opponent at this hearing refused to shake my hand at the end of the debate, and one of the reporters who covered the hearings said I had "eaten my opponents for breakfast." Over time, I have learned to take these encounters less personally. The bill that would have legalized licensed direct-entry midwifery passed with flying colors in the House. After being sent to the Senate floor, the state's medical association's lobby successfully prevented the bill from going to a vote by positioning it as the last piece of business on the agenda for the last day of the session. The midwives of this state have found a sponsor for their bill every year for the last 10 years, and each time they work hard to see it pass and mount an expensive legislative effort, only to watch it die somewhere in the process. At the time of this writing, the midwives of this state continue to attend deliveries at home, engaging in acts of civil disobedience against what they see as an unjust law. They care for an ever-growing number of women and especially for poor and rural mothers, often with little compensation. I testify in this Midwest state when asked, but I am always glad to return to Oregon where many view me as part of the solution, and not part of the problem, in maternal-child health policy reform.

National activists often see Oregon as a Mecca for homebirth because we have a long history of midwifery-friendly legislation. As I discussed in Chapter 6, Oregon is one of only two states that allows voluntary licensure. In 1977, a group of traditional midwives organized a conference that included a talk given by a lawyer who addressed the legal status of homebirth and direct-entry midwifery in the state. Based on the discussions and concerns raised during his presentation, this lawyer wrote to the Attorney General and requested an opinion of law on rules governing the practice of midwifery in Oregon. That opinion held that because birth was not a medical event, but a normal and healthy part of the reproductive years for most women, birth attendants did not have to be nurses or doctors. However, cutting an episiotomy, an incision through the vagina that increases the size of the birth canal, and administering medications were expressly mentioned as practices requiring medical training. In the Attorney General's opinion, direct-entry midwives who attended women at home and did not administer medications or perform episiotomies were practicing within the law.

In 1993, the legislature revisited this opinion and used it as the foundation for a new law initiating a voluntary licensure program in Oregon. The revised law allows licensed direct-entry midwives to carry and administer vital medications and to receive reimbursement from the state Medicaid program called the Oregon Health Plan. As a result of these legal developments, Oregon enjoys some of the most progressive laws of any state, and all direct-entry midwives, licensed or not, who practice at home have some measure of legal protection from their medical model opponents who would like to see homebirth outlawed. Because the Oregon Health Plan covers homebirth services, Oregon midwives are able to attend a high percentage of low-income women, an essential provision because homebirth midwives are sometimes the only viable maternity care option for rural mothers who lack transportation.

Periodically, however, the midwives of Oregon face challenges when legislators propose riders to bills that, if passed, would make licensure mandatory in Oregon. Because of my work with task forces on outcomes of licensed vs. unlicensed midwives discussed in the previous chapter, I am often called to testify at hearings related to mandatory licensure. In addition, for the last two years I have served at the state legislative liaison for the Oregon Midwifery Council, the only professional organization for direct-entry midwives in Oregon. I work with two amazing lobbyists who keep me apprised of challenges to our autonomy and our current licensure status. I have to be ready, often with little warning, to travel to the state capital for hearings and individual meetings with senators and representatives who are sympathetic to the midwifery cause.

While finishing the edits on this book, I was called to one such hearing and asked to discuss the cultural context and political-economic ramifications of mandatory licensure in Oregon. I had just a few hours to prepare. I cut out of office hours early with a scribbled note of apology to students and headed up I-5 through the driving and parking nightmare that is our state capital. I had my own homeborn baby daughter—my secret weapon—in tow. A born politician, she seems to know just when to smile and squeal flirtatiously as a doting Senator or Representative catches her eye. I was scheduled for last on the agenda. Our large contingent of mothers, babies, and midwives waited outside the hearing room until just before our turn. I had been nine months' pregnant the last time I sat before the committee, and as they called me forward, the members of the House Health Care Committee all commented on my baby, the great disarmer and equalizer. They were warm and welcoming, but their questions were serious. Why not just make licensure mandatory in Oregon? The following is my reply.

"Chair Goodwin, members of the committee, I thank you for the opportunity to speak with you today. For the record my name is Melissa Cheyney, and I am an assistant professor of medical anthropology at Oregon State University, Vice-Chair of the Governor's Board of Licensed Direct-Entry Midwifery, a licensed midwife, and as of May 2009, a homebirth consumer. By way of introduction for the public record, I want to start with a brief overview of the role of midwives in global maternal-child health programs. The majority of babies around the world today are born at home attended by a midwife. In low-income nations, midwives work against the insurmountable odds of poverty, chronic infections disease loads, poor nutrition, contaminated water, and lack of access to medical facilities when complications arise. And yet, research has shown midwifery to be a highly effective strategy for reducing perinatal deaths, or deaths that occur right around the time of birth. Most infant deaths today occur in the first year of life and are not related to birth complications, but to respiratory diseases and gastrointestinal infections caused by poor sanitation and polluted water sources."

"In all high-income nations except for the United States, midwives are the primary maternity providers.[1] In response to an increase in the use of midwives as a public health strategy, maternal mortality rates decreased by about 16 percent in all high-income countries, except for the United States, between 2000 and 2005. Here at home, maternal mortality increased by 54 percent during the same time period. The United States also ranks second to worst in perinatal mortality rates among similarly sized high-income countries. All but one of the nations where maternal and infant mortality rates are lower than in the United States have two things in common—universal health care and midwives as the primary providers. These two solutions are linked because universal maternity care is made possible by the lower costs, reduced rates of unnecessary interventions, and improved health outcomes associated with midwifery care. The benefits of in-home midwifery care across cultures and numerous credentialing processes have been clearly documented in over 30 scientific studies."

"Midwifery care is, thus, the norm in both low- and high-income nations—the United States excepted. Oregon, however, has been a national leader in progressive legislation that promotes in-home midwifery care as a solution to the problems of low access and high costs. Oregon and Utah are the only two states in the United States that have voluntary licensure for midwives. These two states have in common a substantial and vocal minority of constituents that see midwifery as a healing art that should not be overly controlled by the state. Oregon and Utah are clear priorities for research that examines the effects of licensure on the safety of home delivery."

"Oregon currently has 55 licensed and 77 unlicensed direct-entry midwives, as ascertained through birth certificate submission records. This means that over half of Oregon midwives are not licensed. Direct-entry midwives in general, but unlicensed ones in particular, are disproportionately serving underserved and rural women in Oregon. A few months ago the Board of Direct-Entry Midwifery voted to endorse a project designed to study homebirth outcomes by provider type—that is, by licensed vs. unlicensed midwife—using 2008 vital records data. 2008 is the first year where planned homebirths were recorded on Oregon birth certificates. I will serve as the primary investigator on the project, and we have already received Institutional Review Board approval from my home institution, Oregon State University, as well as Oregon vital records. However, the

---

1. All of the statistics presented during this testimony came from CIA (2008), Declercq (2009), Save the Children (2007), and WHO (2007).

2008 dataset will not be available to researchers until December 2009. I have provided you with a copy of a preliminary study in one Oregon county where my co-researchers and I found no differences between the birth outcomes achieved by licensed and unlicensed midwives. The 2008 vital records project should help to answer this question more definitively."

"Oregon has a long tradition of support for midwifery and, by extension, the perspectives held by many of your constituents—that birth in normal, healthy, low-risk women is not primarily a medical event. With high-quality, time-intensive prenatal care, midwives are able to determine who can deliver at home and who might be better served by a hospital birth. Homebirth midwives and their clients are not, however, uniform groups. The crux of our current issue—why some midwives get licensed while others do not—can be explained by examining philosophical and economic barriers to licensure, along with diversity in beliefs among homebirth providers and clients."

"A small percentage of direct-entry midwives in Oregon represent minority cultural groups, as with some Native and African America midwives, who are trained by traditional midwives in their own cultural traditions, serving women who share similar cultural values. They see licensure as irrelevant to their practice of traditional midwifery. In addition, some small groups of direct-entry midwives feel called by God to attend women in their churches, and they often feel that it is important to keep midwifery 'out of bed with the state.' Additionally, some midwives see medical monopolies as dangerous, believing that our 'disease-care' system can be refined and held accountable by independent practitioners speaking at the margins. Medical anthropologists refer to the presence of multiple, sometimes competing modalities of healing or treatment as 'medical pluralism,' and we see this as a sign of a healthy system."

"The largest barrier to licensure, however, is not philosophical, but economic. The cost of licensure in Oregon is $1,900 for a two-year period, as compared to medical doctors who pay $200 each year. Given the extraordinary differences in average income between doctors and homebirth midwives, the cost of licensing is absurd and seen by many midwives as a form of not-so-covert suppression."

The committee was disbelieving, and Chair Goodwin stopped my testimony: "$1,900 every two years?"

"Yes, and that is recently down from the $1,500 per year that we paid up until 2008," I explained.

"Why is it so high?" asked another member of the committee.

"We have been told that the health licensing agency that houses our board and oversees our licensing simply divides operating costs by the number of licensees. $1,900 per license is what it takes to oversee licensure."

Chair Goodwin clearly found my answer unsatisfactory and asked if any representative from the Oregon Health Licensing Agency was present. The new director happened to be in the audience, and he came up to the stand. He stated his name for the record and proceeded to explain that the costs were tied to investigating complaints against midwives, suggesting that these were common and expensive to investigate. Chair Goodwin asked how many complaints were filed each year on average, but the director, only seven weeks into his tenure, did not know.

I interrupted: "Chair Goodwin, if I may, I serve on the enforcement committee that reviews all complaints and makes recommendations for remediation and the suspension of licenses when necessary. I serve with two other board members, and we are all volunteers. We receive five to six complaints per year, and we take action on an average of one per year."

"One per year?" Goodwin seemed frustrated. "Director, you will get back to us with a full report justifying the costs of licensure for direct-entry midwives. I would like to see them pay no more that $200 per year. Dr. Cheyney, please continue with your testimony."[2]

"In closing, Chair Goodwin, members of the committee, my recommendation is that you delay any action on mandatory licensure until we have the safety evidence from the 2008 vital records study. In the meantime, I request that you work with the board to make licensure more attractive by improving access to courses required for licensing, decreasing fees, and developing a religious and cultural exemption clause that gives immunity to midwives who represent minority religious and cultural groups. It will take time to overhaul this 16-year-old system of voluntary licensure, and that overhaul should be evidence-based. A lot is at stake for the women and families of Oregon. This debate is primarily about safety, but I would like to remind the committee that it is not only about safety. It is also about a woman's right to choose where and with whom she gives birth. It is about access to care, affordability, and using allied health professionals such as direct-entry midwives to reduce our state's maternal and infant health disparities. Thank you for your time."

The committee voted to table all discussion and legislation regarding mandatory licensure until they could discuss the licensing fee issue. Thirty minutes of testimony and questioning and the legislative threat to the 77 unlicensed midwives in Oregon, a threat that would have criminalized them, was gone—at least in the short term. A small number of fellow academics with similar research interests read the articles we publish in peer-reviewed journals, and few of these articles ever lead to substantial social or policy change. The applied work of medical anthropology includes serving on public health task forces, testifying before state and federal legislators, and serving on boards that write the administrative rules that govern practice for a group of health care providers; these are just a few of the ways applied medical anthropologists see their work making a difference.

MATERNITY CARE REFORM:
THE NEED TO BEGIN AT HOME

During meetings with legislators and policymakers, in response to my critiques of contemporary approaches to birthing care in the United States, they often ask me what I would do differently. Sometimes the asker really wants to know and

---

2. "After this testimony, the director of the agency that oversees the Board of Direct-Entry Midwifery worked tirelessly to change the fee structure for midwives. As this book goes to print, the fees have been reduced to just over $600 per year!"

sometimes the question is a challenge with the subtext being: "Yes, there are problems, but I'd like to see you come up with a better solution." I actually have an answer to this question, and it revolves around a concept called hegemony and the sense of responsibility deriving from my travels to low-income nations. Hegemony, as mentioned in Chapter 3, means rule by cultural consent, and it refers to how specific practices, ideas, and values gain acceptance because they are associated with a cultural group or nation that holds power. All around the world, viable systems of ethnomedicine and indigenous healing traditions have been undermined by beliefs in the power and efficacy of Western-style, for-profit biomedicine. Whether biomedicine is truly superior is irrelevant; what matters is how people perceive it. Medical anthropologists have written extensively about the hegemony of biomedicine, noting that because it has an aura of superiority, it has been exported and implemented with varying degrees of effectiveness all around the world. As an anthropologist working on the problem of poor maternal and infant health outcomes and inequality in access to birthing care, I believe we have a responsibility to make sure that the system we advocate for in the United States is actually one worth emulating around the world.

I have a vision of a four-tiered, midwifery-dominated maternity system where all healthy women begin their pregnancies with a visit to a midwife, either direct-entry or certified nurse, and plan for a home or birth-center delivery. Women who develop risk factors or come with preexisting conditions would transfer to a second tier of care with a certified nurse midwife who has hospital privileges and is closer to a collaborating physician. Most women would deliver at one of these two levels of care. However, if more difficult-to-treat complications arise over the course of prenatal care, a small percentage of women might need to transfer to a third tier managed by obstetricians, or even on to a fourth tier of specialists called perinatologists who deal with rare and occasionally life-threatening conditions of pregnancy. Women would begin at the most basic level of primary care with midwives and only move to a hospital-based certified nurse midwife or to care with physicians if medically indicated. Fewer and fewer women would require care as we move up toward the fourth tier, which is also the most expensive. This means that only midwives would attend low-risk women, allocating physicians to treat high-risk pregnancies. Obstetricians who want to attend normal, low-risk women could do so, but only after successfully completing a normal birth internship overseen by an experienced midwife or similarly credentialed physician.

Low-risk women who have had healthy pregnancies would go through labor at home or in an independent birth center, and only transport to the hospital in case of a complication during labor or following delivery. Certified nurse midwives could assist with most initial hospital transports, especially for those involving slow, nonprogressive labors resulting from a poorly positioned forward-facing infant. In such cases, the mother might only need an epidural to allow her to rest and a touch of pitocin to increase the strength of contractions and speed labor. If these interventions were to fail, an obstetrician could be called to perform a cesarean delivery. Midwives, obstetricians, and perinatologists would collaborate, providing continuity of care for women who move to higher tiers due to heightened risk factors. Occasionally, after successful medical intervention, women could return to care at a lower tier.

This system would require mutual respect as well as an infrastructure for information sharing between tiers of providers and across birth settings. Clear guidelines for referral would be developed by mixed boards of midwives, obstetricians, and pediatricians; tested for their effectiveness; and modified as needed. This arrangement would also require mutual respect for midwifery and medical models of care. Physicians and midwives would have to begin to see each other as valuable colleagues with unique perspectives and experiences if articulations are to be smooth and not fractured. Midwives would be acknowledged as the specialists in normal birth, and obstetricians as surgical experts who are adept at handling the high-risk deliveries, especially those that cannot occur vaginally.

Medical anthropologists would have an important role to play in this four-tiered system of birthing care because midwives and doctors would need cultural brokers and translators to help bridge the philosophical and experiential divide between them, at least initially. Respect for different kinds of skills and views of birth should be recast as issues of cultural competency, with emphasis on providers across the maternity care spectrum acquiring the knowledge and skills needed for working in an environment of birthing care pluralism.

If 70–75 percent of women could deliver with midwives either at home, in independent birth centers, or in the hospital, and if obstetricians and perinatologists could manage the other 25–30 percent, the cost savings would mean that all women and babies could have access to high-quality birthing care. Today the average cost of an uncomplicated vaginal birth in the hospital is about $8,000, while cesareans are approximately $15,000 and neither of these costs includes prenatal or postpartum care. Homebirth midwives charge from $2,000 to $4,000 on average, and their fees generally include all prenatal, postpartum, and well-baby care from conception through six weeks postpartum. Midwifery-dominated systems save money while improving outcomes by decreasing the rate of unnecessary interventions and the negative side effects they carry. Midwives and physicians would redefine "positive outcomes" holistically, working together to produce healthy babies and also to make sure that as many women as possible reflect back on their birth experiences and describe them as empowering and transformative. Online support groups for survivors of birth trauma and unnecessary cesareans would no longer be one of the fastest growing internet communities.

Dreams of reform notwithstanding, the current, for-profit health care system, and especially the astronomical costs of high-ticket items such as maternal-child health, contribute to an international embarrassment. The United States currently spends more than half of the entire world's health care dollars, leaving other nations to share smaller and smaller pieces of the pie. Women in the United States pay $15,000 on average for their unnecessary cesareans, while women in Africa die from hemorrhages that cost less than one dollar and a clean syringe to treat. Our role as a world power carries with it an ethical responsibility to think about the interconnections of our increasingly global society. How we perform birth here deeply influences what happens in other places around the world. Medical anthropology, with its holistic, cross-cultural, and evolutionary foci, is uniquely positioned to address issues of hegemony and biomedical domination and to help broker the changes that would make our health care system one worth emulating. The transition from high-tech, high-cost obstetrics to a four-tiered system with clear guidelines for referral and a focus on prevention over intervention will help to decrease expenditures and improve outcomes, allowing valuable health care dollars now being wasted to go to those truly in need. I wrote President Obama to tell him about my idea. He hasn't gotten back to me yet.

REFOCUSING UPSTREAM

I conclude this book with an often-repeated parable in public health circles that is particularly germane to debates over the future of maternal and infant health care reform in the United States. In one version of the tale, two physicians are sitting along the edge of a swiftly moving river when they see an infant drowning in the powerful current. One physician jumps in and pulls the child to safety, administering artificial respiration. As she works to resuscitate the first baby, another one floats by, and the second physician jumps in attempting to save him. Just as each infant begins to recover and breathe spontaneously, another drowning child is swept by on the raging current, and both physicians work furiously to try to save as many babies as possible. Finally, near exhaustion, one of the physicians begins to run upstream away from the backlog of drowning infants. The downstream doctor calls out in desperation, "Where are you going?" and hears in response, "I am going to see who the hell is throwing all of these babies into the river!"

   The point of this tale is that resources and practices excessively devoted to "downstream" endeavors are often heroic but also inefficient, expensive, superficial, and ultimately insufficient for preventing or reducing the number of individuals thrown into the river to begin with. While they give the impression of effort and significant investment in health care, they often do not effectively solve more systemic and institutionalized problems such as inadequacies in access to care and declining overall health, closely tied to socioeconomic status and issues of gender inequity and poverty. McKinley (1986), the medical anthropologist often attributed with the first version of this parable, asserts that biomedicine should curtail its excessive preoccupation with high-tech solutions and short-term tinkering and begin to refocus upstream on the origins of problems.

   In my version of the story, obstetricians begin to argue over what kinds of high-tech respirators can best oxygenate the highest number of drowning victims in the shortest amount of time while avoiding lawsuits. The midwives question whether full resuscitation was truly necessary and whether an herb or alternative therapy might work just as well with fewer side effects, while affirming the baby's role in choosing to live. Biological anthropologists collect data on the infants' core temperatures and rates of recovery and organize a panel on adaptive responses to hypothermia in newborn drowning victims. The cultural anthropologists deconstruct what it means to come close to asphyxiation in a society that so deeply values breathing, while examining the ways unequal relations of power are reproduced in the disparate treatment of drowning victims according to ethnicity. This flurry of research produces a façade of engagement, and still no one hikes upstream.

Obstetricians assign the diagnosis of "failure to progress" to laboring women who dilate or push only to a point and then experience a slowing or an arrest of progress toward delivery. This is the most common diagnosis in obstetrics, and physicians often use it to justify interventions such as pitocin augmentation and cesarean section. Ironically, the threat of these interventions and a model that pathologizes normal peaks and lulls in labor patterns may be contributing to the very halt in progression that it seeks to correct. In this way, "failure to progress" represents a metaphor for the current system of birthing care in the United States. We can turn, refocus upstream, challenge the entire foundation of biomedical and technocratic approaches, and work to redefine normal in the birthplace, or we can continue our downstream endeavors and risk the diagnosis of chronic, irresolvable "failure to progress."

POSTCRIPT: A WHOLE NEW LEVEL OF PARTICIPANT-OBSERVATION

On May 4, 2009, I was exactly 38 weeks pregnant. I had been working long 14- to 16-hour days trying to finish up a spring term writing grant that had allowed me to complete a draft of my book. I also had several current midwifery clients. I was hoping to squeeze in as many births as I could before my own delivery so that I could take a hiatus from midwifery after giving birth and still keep my client numbers high enough to justify the cost of my license. I was looking so forward to the 4th because that was the date when I had planned to slow down, rest, and get ready for the baby to come. I had one mother left who still needed to deliver before me, and she was due any day. As I relaxed on the couch that night reflecting on how excited I was to have some downtime, I had a sudden and strong intuition that someone was going to go into labor that night. I had my husband help load all of my birth equipment into the car so that I would not have to pack it all up in the wee hours of the morning when I would surely be called.

I fell asleep on the coach reading a book at about midnight and slept deeply until pain in my back woke me around 3 a.m. I rolled over on the couch and slept restlessly, through the haze of my tiredness, dimly aware of pain in my back. At 4:30 in the morning I woke up and started walking toward my bedroom. As I climbed the stairs, contractions came on like a freight train, hitting every two to three minutes, dropping me to my knees and breaking my water. I woke my husband Andy with my "birth song." He sat up dazed in bed: "What's going on?" I said I thought I might be in labor and that I thought my water had broken. "You think? Don't you know? You're a midwife! What do I do? I don't have a substitute lined up for class today. You said first-time mothers almost always go overdue. You can't have the baby today." Another contraction, stronger than the last, came, and I was screaming: "Rub my back! My back! Oh god, my back. What the hell? The baby is facing forward. I knew it! Damn it! You have to turn around little baby."

In between contractions, I called my midwifery assistant and asked her if she could handle my prenatal visits that day. I instructed her to keep my labor a secret until I had delivered the baby. I had felt so under the microscope during my pregnancy. Many well-meaning people made stress-inducing comments: "Wow, wouldn't it be crazy if you ended up with a cesarean after all of your research?" Or, "what if you have to transport?" "What if after all of your work on natural birth, you end up getting pain medications?" None of these comments were helpful, and the hardest thing about my pregnancy was definitely the mental work of putting other people's commentary aside as I tried to enjoy the experience. My midwives helped me to process the pressures and to set some of that baggage aside, but the sense of being onstage came back with the start of contractions—until the excruciating pain in my back removed all thoughts of anything else.

My midwives, Colleen and Carla, arrived around 8:30 in the morning and attempted to talk me down off the ledge about my baby's position. I knew too much, and I kept thinking, as a first-time mom with a forward-facing baby, I am 34 times more likely to transport to the hospital. They reminded me that it was not a problem unless it was a problem, and that my labor seemed to be progressing well. I was strong and committed, and I could do this. Colleen checked me soon after they arrived, and I was already five centimeters dilated. That seemed like relatively quick progress given the baby's position. Maybe if I got to complete dilation before exhaustion set in, I could push the baby down far enough that she would rotate at the pelvic outlet. Clinically speaking, things went smoothly for the next few hours, though I was not performing labor the way I had hoped. No quiet, focused breathing through the contractions, no surrendering to the pain, no candles, soft music, or letting my body do it. I was screaming and swearing like a sailor: "My back! My back! Holy shit! My back! Rub my back!"

Colleen, Carla, and Andy took turns holding my hands, pressing on my back, and encouraging me to walk and change position. I climbed the stairs, got in and out of the birthing tub, and complained as loudly as I possibly could, using the F-word as my birth mantra at the peak of every contraction. Through it all, I was distantly aware of getting to experience so many of the sensations I had witnessed in my clients: back labor, exhaustion, wondering if I could do it, hoping that the baby was OK. I had asked the midwives to listen to the baby's heartbeat through earphones. I knew that the sound would move me out of my birthing mother space and into midwife mode, assessing safety and evaluating fetal well-being. They honored my request, and I felt that it allowed me to get out of my conscious mind and into laborland where I could do what I needed to do.

Around 3:00 in the afternoon my cervix was completely dilated, and it was time to start pushing. The baby was high and still facing forward, and I knew I had a lot of work to do to bring her down. I pushed for three hours in every position we could think of and made little progress. The midwives were encouraging, but I could tell I was not making progress, and my uterus was starting to tire. Contractions were lighter and spacing out. I ate, drank, and took several herbal concoctions to help restore my energy and increase the strength of my contractions. At some point, it was clear that I would just have to gut out the pushing, relying primarily on my abdominal muscles. My confidence faltered, and I told Colleen that I didn't think I could do it. She said, "You've only been pushing for three hours, the baby sounds great, you're healthy and strong. You have a lot more in there. You have dig down deep inside to find the strength you need to continue."

Things turned the corner over the next few hours as I pushed in a squat leaning against the edge of the tub as Andy and Carla grasped arms and pushed against my hips as hard as they could, trying to open the pelvic outlet and give the baby space to rotate. "God damned, piece of shit hip squeeze! I can't believe I'm getting the hip squeeze! Please turn, baby. Please, get out of my back!" Legs cramping, trembling with fatigue, sun setting, I kept pushing. At the five-hour mark, while squatting during a hip squeeze, a contraction started that was harder and longer than the ones my tired uterus had been churning out before, and at the peak of it, pushing with all I had, I felt the baby's head rotate and begin to descend in the birth canal. I let out a blood-curdling scream that brought Colleen up from the basement where she had been heating towels in the dryer. "Now we're going to have a baby," she said. I pushed for another hour, finally making progress. I felt the baby start to crown, and I walked over to the birth stool. I looked down at Andy whose eyes were glassy with tears as he sat waiting to catch our baby. The craziness and intensity of the day melted away and it was just the three of us, suspended in time, an incredible cosmic moment that I will never forget. I reached down, pushing into my own hand, finally feeling her head and knowing I would be holding my baby soon. I felt her head emerge, and then her little body twisted slowly as her shoulders cleared the bones. She dropped into her daddy's waiting hands, and Andy sobbed as he caught her, looked her over, and passed her up into my arms. We held her together, kissing and nuzzling and laughing as she gradually came into her body after that most difficult journey. She opened her eyes and stared intently at me. We watched her little body turn pink as she took her first breath—a warm rosiness starting first over her heart and then slowly spreading out across her body as she began to wiggle and coo and sputter, clearing her own airway. I can't imagine anything ever topping those first few moments with her. The relief and joy were definitely proportional to the pain and exertion that had consumed me just minutes before.

Colleen monitored my blood loss and helped the placenta to deliver while Carla watched over our baby. Andy and I just stared in awe. At some point, we remembered that we didn't know the sex. For a while she was just a baby, and neither of us had thought to check. Andy looked and announced what I had felt all along—a baby girl! She weighed 7 lbs ands 3 oz and was born at 8:52 p.m. after six hours of grueling pushing and 10 hours of back labor. The best part is that she was born on May 5—International Midwives Day! We named her Ninkasi after the Sumerian goddess of beer. My husband is a middle school world history teacher and an amateur brewer. She has a little bit of each of us in her.

Colleen and Carla cleaned up, performed the newborn exam, fed us, and tucked us into bed for our first night together. Throughout the night, Andy and I kept waking up, staring at her, and talking about the birth. We were both elated. It's hard to put into words the joy and magic of my birth and our first few days and weeks together as a new family. It was surreal and intoxicating and without a doubt the most transformative, pushed-to-the-limit, triumphant, summitting-Mt. Everest experience of my life to date. The hard work and pain were so worth it, and Ninkasi's birth, more than anything else, renewed my commitment to homebirth as a political movement. I understand better than ever the women who choose to give birth at home even in an illegal state, the women so committed to experiencing unmedicated birth on their own terms that they drive for hours to see midwives in other states because they can't find one to attend them where they live, and the mothers who, feeling scarred and disempowered by their hospital births, are determined to do something different the next time.

I also felt proud of being a midwife and a bearer of the specialized knowledge preserved and passed down through generations of oppressed and persecuted midwives who continue to serve women even at great cost to themselves. Low-tech, time-honored strategies for rectifying Ninkasi's position had worked for me, and I renewed my commitment to see other women begin their families the way I did—on top of the world! Most of all, I felt gratitude to my little Ninkasi who has taught me more than anyone else about midwifery models of care and why some women choose, against all odds, to give birth at home. To you and your daddy, I dedicate this book.

Appendix A

Risk Index Criteria

	Risk Assessment Factor
Absolute Risk Criteria (24)	Active Cancer*
	Cardiac Disease*
	Severe Renal Disease*
	Severe Liver Disease*
	Uncontrolled Hyperthyroidism*
	Chronic Obstructive Pulmonary Disease*
	Essential Chronic Hypertension*
	Pre-eclampsia/Eclampsia*
	Thrombophelbitis*
	Substance abuse known to cause adverse effects (tobacco, alcohol, illicit drug use)*
	Incomplete Spontaneous Abortion*
	Hemoglobin <9 at term*
	Placental Abruption*
	Placental Previa at onset of labor*
	Persistent, severe abnormal quantity of amniotic fluid*
	Blood Coagulation Defect*
	Amnionitis*
	Pregnancy >43 weeks*
	Pregnancy >42 weeks with abnormal non-stress test*
	Pregnancy with abnormal fetal surveillance test*
	Rupture of membranes >72 hours before onset of labor with chorioamnionitis*

(continued)

	Risk Assessment Factor
	Secondary herpes that cannot be covered at onset of labor*
	HIV-positive status with AIDS*
	Higher order multiples (3 or more)*
Non-Absolute Risk Criteria (15)	Conditions requiring ongoing medical supervision or ongoing use of medications
	Significant glucose intolerance
	Inappropriate fetal size for gestation
	Significant 2nd or 3rd trimester bleeding
	Abnormal fetal cardiac rate or rhythm or decrease of fetal movement
	Uterine Anomaly
	Anemia (Hematocrit <30 at term)
	Seizure disorder requiring prescriptive medication
	Platelet Count <75,000
	Previous uterine incision other than low transverse cesarean and/or myomectomy with review of surgical records and/or subsequent birth history
	Isoimmunization to blood factors
	Psychiatric Disorders
	History of thrombophelbitis and hemoglobinopathies
	Twin Gestation
	Malpresentation at term
Additional Risk Criteria (25)	Inadequate Prenatal Care
	Month prenatal care began (late to care)
	Number of prenatal visits
	Low 1-minute Apgar score
	Low 5-minute Apgar score
	Estimated gestation <37 weeks or >42 weeks
	Maternal age <18 years
	Maternal age >34 years
	Risk Factor Count
	No Antepartum Procedures
	Abnormal Amniocentesis
	Tocolysis
	No Ultrasound
	No antepartum procedure history

(continued)

Risk Assessment Factor
Antepartum Procedure other
Antepartum Procedure ICD other
No Intrapartum Procedures
Inadequate Intrapartum Monitoring
Previous Pregnancy Loss
Neonatal Intensive Care
Newborn Death
Newborn Transferred
Previous Infant >4,000 grams
Previous Preterm Infant
Rh Sensitization

*Indicates an absolute risk-factor as defined by the Oregon Administrative Rules (OAR) of the Oregon Board of Direct-Entry Midwifery

Appendix B

Policy for Increased Collaboration Between Direct-Entry Midwives (DEMs) and Obstetricians for Homebirth Clients

MELISSA CHEYNEY, PHD, CPM, LDM
Oregon State University
Department of Anthropology

and

PAUL QUALTERRE-BURCHER, MD, MA
Doctoral Student
University of Oregon
Department of Philosophy

GOALS

1. To improve communication and collaboration between direct-entry midwives and physicians.
2. To help create a climate of mutual respect and understanding between practitioners of midwifery and medical models of care.
3. To design and implement protocols to facilitate transports, transfers of care, and co-care consultations between direct-entry midwives and physicians.

CONTEXT

- Homebirth is a safe alternative to hospital birth for most women particularly when attended by skilled, experienced direct-entry midwives with access to physician back-up.

- Research clearly supports homebirth as a viable option for low-risk women, though many physicians remain skeptical or explicitly opposed to this option either due to a lack of awareness of the literature or because they have been influenced by their own or their colleagues' experiences with transport (i.e., anecdotal data).

- Obstetricians and hospital care represent a "safety net" that often allows for positive outcomes even when a homebirth client develops complications.

- Better cooperation between direct-entry midwives and obstetricians will improve outcomes in these complicated situations by facilitating continuity of care through keeping the midwife involved in the care of her client, enhancing communication between providers, and allowing for interventions available only in the hospital under obstetric or certified nurse midwife (CNM) care.

- Research has identified two areas where morbidity and mortality are increased in a homebirth sample: breech and twins. For example, the Johnson and Daviss (2005) study showed a doubling of mortality rate when twins and breeches were included. In addition, given the elevated risk associated with some Vaginal Birth After Cesarean (VBAC) scenarios, postdates beyond 42 weeks, gestational diabetes, pre-eclampsia, and other conditions, homebirth midwives may find themselves in need of a consulting physician.

  - In some areas of Oregon, direct-entry midwives, and especially new direct-entry midwives, find access to physician backup difficult or impossible.

  - Direct-entry midwives may benefit from a more formalized protocol allowing them access to physician consultation. However, it is clear under Oregon law that direct-entry midwives remain autonomous practitioners and that the ultimate decision to consult or transfer care lies with our birthing families. However, the decision to seek consultation may benefit both families and practitioners when higher risk conditions are present.

  - Additionally, following research conducted by the Oregon Health Licensing Agency in 2009 that examined complaints brought against licensed direct-entry midwives (LDMs), complications associated with breech, twins, VBAC, and postdates are overrepresented in the last 15 years of complaints. Hostility between home and hospital providers and a resulting lack of options for the mother and family played a role in most, if not all, of these cases.

  - Because no information provided to a client is ever completely value free, there may be some benefit to homebirth clientele to hearing multiple perspectives on risks associated with breech, twins, VBACs, postdates, etc. If mothers still choose to pursue a homebirth after consulting with a physician for a higher-risk birth, the midwife may be protected from the accusation that true informed consent was not obtained. Accusations against the midwife regarding lack of informed consent also predominate in the complaints filed against licensed direct-entry midwives in the last 15 years.

- Physicians may benefit from prenatal consultation with homebirth clients who are higher risk because they have the opportunity to meet the woman and her family prior to a possible intrapartum transport. This will also allow physicians to understand the extent to which homebirth practice is dictated by the worldviews of the minority of families who choose an out-of-hospital birth, reducing accusations that midwives misrepresent risks to their clients.

- Acknowledging that smooth articulations between home and hospital providers remain a utopian ideal, we have collaborated on this proposal in an effort to at least begin a dialogue.

PROPOSAL

We recommend that:

1. Obstetricians acknowledge that there are over 30 studies that now clearly indicate homebirth as a safe and viable option for low-risk women.

2. Direct-entry midwives acknowledge that their views of the hospital and their models of care are disproportionately affected by those clients who have had negative experiences in the hospital and are therefore seeking homebirth care as an alternative. This would entail the acknowledgment that many hospital-based providers are working diligently to humanize birth.

3. Providers already familiar with and supportive of the larger worldviews that inform the midwifery model of care take responsibility for initiating a cultural shift in the hospital environment that promotes mutual respect between obstetricians and direct-entry midwives.

4. All home and hospital-based providers suspend judgment and stereotypes and work to have a better understanding of the worldviews, cultural values, institutional barriers, and the needs of various patient/client populations that affect the provision of care under each model.

5. Direct-entry midwives and obstetricians acknowledge the choices surrounding place of birth constitute cultural differences. The same respect and cultural sensitivity offered to women with cultural, language, or religious differences should be extended to practitioners and their clients/patients who hold potentially opposing perspectives on childbirth.

6. Direct-entry midwives seek outpatient consultation with an obstetrician of their choice when faced with higher risk circumstances that include, but are not limited to, breech, twins, VBAC, and postdates (remembering that the ultimate decision to consult lies with our birthing families). Direct-entry midwives also require access to collaborating physicians for mundane complications of pregnancy such as bladder infections and resistant yeast infections. We recommend that willing obstetricians work to make prenatal consultation and collaboration more readily available.

7. The goal of consultation will depend on the circumstances, but will in many cases include an offer from the obstetrician to transfer care for the birth to a hospital setting. Whenever this occurs, every effort should be made to honor the maternal-midwife connection and to maintain continuity of care (i.e., keeping the midwife involved as a colleague throughout the intrapartum period).

8. If the homebirth client accepts the counseling of the physician, the physician's group will become jointly responsible for that client provided she continues within the care plan as outlined together.

9. If the homebirth client does not develop a jointly agreed-on care plan with the obstetrician, then that obstetrician and group are not responsible for that client if she should require emergent transfer to the hospital during or after birth. Should transport result in this scenario, the patients do not lose any rights to access to care that they would have held before consult, i.e., access to physician on call for the undoctored. Practitioners will work to maintain mutual respect and communication even during this potentially contentious scenario.

10. If a transport from home to hospital is required during labor or in the immediate postpartum period for women who have not consulted previously because of their low-risk status, the midwife should be able to call the hospital and be told who the physician on call is. Whenever possible, we also recommend that the midwife be given contact information for the on-call doctor so that the reasons for transport can be discussed before the client arrives at the hospital. Further, if the physician and midwife can meet and discuss the reasons for transport in the hall prior to entering the room, an agreed-on plan of action can be offered to the client in a way that communicates midwife and obstetrician collaboration rather than opposition. Because transport is almost always difficult for the family, a positive and mutually respectful working relationship between midwife and obstetrician can help to mitigate the stress and disappointment of a transport and increase the likelihood of a positive outcome/birth experience for the family.

11. On a quarterly basis, physicians and midwives meet to discuss transports and transfers of care so that remaining questions or concerns may be addressed openly. This may provide an opportunity for both physician and midwife to learn about and come to respect alternative viewpoints or approaches. This may also improve collaboration in subsequent cases.

12. Opportunities be made available for physicians to observe homebirths and for direct-entry midwives to observe low-risk hospital deliveries. This may increase awareness regarding differences in standards of care in each setting. This may also help to overturn outdated stereotypes of the midwifery and medical models of care, respectively.

13. Finally, a work group be established to continue to dialogue, create, and implement an experimental protocol for collaboration across midwifery and medical models of care.

References

Abrahams, R. (1973). *Ritual for fun and profit (or the ends and outs of celebration).* Paper presented at the Burg Wartenstein Symposium No. 59, Ritual: Reconciliation and Change.

Ahmed, S. M., Beck, B., Maurana, C. A., & Newton, G. (2004). Overcoming barriers to effective community-based participatory research in U.S. medical schools. *Education for Health, 17*(2), 141–151.

Althabe, F., Sosa, C., Belizán, J. M., Gibbons, L., Jacquerioz, F., & Bergel, E. (2006). Cesarean section rates and maternal and neonatal mortality. *Birth, 33*(4), 270–277.

American College of Obstetricians and Gynecologists (ACOG). (2006). *ACOG statement of policy: Out-of-hospital births in the United States.* Washington, D.C.: Author.

ACOG. (2008). *ACOG statement on home births.* Washington, D.C.: Author.

American Medical Association (AMA). (2008). *Resolution 205 on home deliveries.* Chicago: Author.

Angier, N. 1999. *Woman: An Intimate Geography.* New York: Houghton Mifflin.

Armelagos, G., Brown, P., & Turner, B. (2005). Evolutionary, historical and political economic perspectives on health and disease. *Social Science and Medicine, 61*(4), 755–765.

Babcock, B. (Ed.). (1978). *The reversible world: Symbolic inversion in art and society.* Ithaca, NY: Cornell University Press.

Bell, C. (1997). *Ritual perspectives and dimensions.* Oxford: Oxford University Press.

Biesele, B. (1997). An ideal of unassisted birth: Hunting, healing, and transformation among the Kalahari Ju/'hoansi. In R. Davis-Floyd & C. Sargent (Eds.), *Childbirth and authoritative knowledge: Cross cultural perspectives* (pp. 474–499). Berkeley: University of California Press.

Bodner-Alder, B., Bodner, K., Kimberger, O., Lozanov, P., Husslein, P., & Mayerhofer, K. (2003). Women's position during labour: Influence on maternal and neonatal outcome. *Wiener Klinische Wochenschrift, 115* (19–20), 720–723.

Boucher, D., Bennett, C., McFarlin, B., & Freeze, R. (2009). Staying home to give birth: Why women in the

United States choose home birth. *Journal of Midwifery and Women's Health, 54*, 119–126.

Brody, H. (2000). The placebo response: Recent research and implications for family medicine. *The Journal of Family Practice, 49*(7), 649–654.

Brown, Peter J. (Ed.). (1998). *Understanding and applying medical anthropology.* Mountain View, CA: Mayfield Publishing Company.

Bury, M. (1982). Chronic illness as biographical disruption. *Society of Health and Illness, 4*, 167–182.

Butler, J. (1997). *The psychic life of power: Theories in subjection.* Stanford: Stanford University Press.

Cargo, M., & Mercer, S. L. (2008). The value and challenges of participatory research: Strengthening its practice. *Annual Review of Public Health, 29*, 325–350.

Central Intelligence Agency (CIA). 2008. *CIA world factbook.* Washington, D.C.: Author.

Cesario, S. (2004). Reevaluation of Friedman's labor curve: A pilot study. *Journal of Obstetric, Gynecologic, and Neonatal Nursing, 33*(6), 713–722.

Cheyney, M. (2005). *In transition: A biocultural analysis of homebirth midwifery in the United States* (Unpublished doctoral dissertation). University of Oregon, Eugene.

Cheyney, M., & Everson, C. (2009, March). Narratives of risk: Speaking across the hospital/homebirth divide. *Anthropology Newsletter*, 7–9.

Craven, C. (2007). "Consumer's right" to choose a midwife: Shifting meanings for reproductive rights under neoliberalism. *American Anthropologist, 109*(4), 701–712.

Crawford, P. (1990). The construction and experience of maternity in seventeenth-century England. In V. Fildes (Ed.), *Women as mothers in pre-industrial England* (pp. 3–38). London: Routledge.

Crews, D., & Gerber, L. (2008). Genes, geographic ancestry, and disease susceptibility: Applications of evolutionary medicine to clinical settings. In W. Trevathan, E. O. Smith, & J. McKenna (Eds.), *Evolutionary medicine and health: New perspectives* (pp. 368–381). New York: Oxford University Press.

Cunningham, G. F., Leveno, K. L., Bloom, S. L., Hauth, J. C., Gilstrap III, L. C., & Wenstrom, K. D. (2005). *Williams Obstetrics* (22nd ed.). New York: McGraw-Hill.

Davis-Floyd, R. (1992). *Birth as an American rite of passage.* Berkeley: University of California Press.

Davis-Floyd, R. (1994a). Mind over body: The pregnant professional. In N. Sault (Ed.), *Many mirrors: Body image and social relations in anthropological perspective* (pp. 204–233). New Brunswick: Rutgers University Press.

Davis-Floyd, R. (1994b). The technocratic body: American childbirth as cultural expression. *Social Science and Medicine, 38*(8), 1125–1140.

Davis-Floyd, R. (1997). Intuition as authoritative knowledge in midwifery and homebirth. In R. Davis-Floyd & C. Sargent (Eds.), *Childbirth as authoritative knowledge: Cross-cultural perspectives* (pp. 315–349). Berkeley: University of California Press.

Davis-Floyd, R. (2001). The technocratic, humanistic, and holistic paradigms of childbirth. *International Journal of Gynecology and Obstetrics, 75*(1), D5–S23.

Davis-Floyd, R. (2003). Home-birth emergencies in the U.S. and Mexico: The trouble with transport. *Social Science and Medicine, 56*, 1911–1931.

Davis-Floyd, R. (2004). *Birth as an American rite of passage* (2nd ed.). Berkeley and London: University of California Press.

Davis-Floyd, R., & Cheyney, M. (2009). Birth and the big bad wolf: An evolutionary perspective. In H. Selin & P. K. Stone (Eds.), *Childbirth across cultures* (pp. 1–22). Dordrecht, The Netherlands: Springer Publishers.

Davis-Floyd, R., & Davis, E. (1997). Intuition as authoritative knowledge in midwifery and homebirth. In R. Davis-Floyd & P. Sven Arvidson (Eds.), *Intuition: The inside story* (pp. 145–176). New York: Routledge.

Davis-Floyd, R., & St. John, G. (1998). *From doctor to healer: The transformative journey.* New Brunswick: Rutgers University Press.

Declercq, E. (2009). Birth by the numbers. Retrieved from http://www.orgasmicbirth.com/birth-by-the-numbers

Declercq, E. 2007. Trends in CNM Attended Births, 1990–2004. *Journal of Midwifery and Women's Health 52*(1), 87–88.

Declercq, E., Barger, M., Cabral, H., Evans, S., Kotelchuck, M., Simon, S., Weiss, J., & Heffner, L. (2007). Maternal outcomes associated with planned primary cesareans compared to planned vaginal births. *Obstetrics and Gynecology, 109*(3), 669–677.

de Jonge, A., van der Goes, B., Ravelli, A., Amelink-Verburg, M., Mol, B., Nijhuis, J., Bennebroek Gravenhorst, J., & Buitendijk, S. (2009). Perinatal mortality and morbidity in a nationwide cohort of 529,688 low-risk planned home and hospital births. *International Journal of Obstetrics and Gynecology, 116*(9), 1177–1184.

DeVries, R. (2004). *A pleasing birth: Midwives and maternity care in the Netherlands.* Philadelphia: Temple University Press.

Diegmann, E., Andrews, C., & Niemczura, C. (2000). The length of the second stage of labor in uncomplicated, nulliparous African American and Puerto Rican women. *Journal of Midwifery and Women's Health, 45*(1), 67–71.

Dominguez, T. P. (2008). Race, racism, and racial disparities in adverse birth outcomes. *Clinical Obstetrics and Gynecology, 51*(2): 360–370.

Downe, S., Ed. (2004). *Normal childbirth: Evidence and debate.* Edinburgh: Churchill Livingstone.

Eaton, S. B., Eaton III, S. B., & Cordain, L. (2002). Evolution, diet, and health. In P. S. Ungar & M. F. Teaford (Eds.), *Human diet: Its origin and evolution* (pp. 7–17). Westport, CT: Bergin and Garvey.

Emhamed, M., van Rheenen, P., & Brabin, B. (2004). The early effects of delayed cord clamping in term infants born to Libyan mothers. *Tropical Doctor, 34*(4), 218–222.

Evans, D. (2005). Suppression of the acute-phase response as a biological mechanism for the placebo effect. *Medical Hypotheses, 64*(1), 1–7.

Felix Aaron, K., & Stryer, D. (2003). Moving from rhetoric to evidence-based action in health care. *Journal of General and Internal Medicine, 18*, 589–591.

Fischler, N., Kasehagen, L., Rosenberg, K., Nute Wiens, H., & Yusem, S. (2007). *Perinatal data book.* Portland: Oregon Department of Human Services.

Friedman, E. (1955). Primigravid labor: A graphicostatistical analysis. *Obstetrics and Gynecology, 6*(6), 567–589.

Friedman, E. (1967). *Labor: Clinical evaluation and management.* New York: Appleton-Century Crofts.

Foucault, M. (1979). *Discipline and punish: Birth of the prison.* New York: Vintage Books.

Foucault, M. (1982). The subject and the power. In H. Dreyfus & P. Rabinow (Eds.), *Beyond structuralism and hermeneutics*. New York: Harvester Wheatsheaf.

Fullerton, J., Navarro, A., & Young, S. (2007). Outcomes of planned home births: An integrative review. *Journal of Midwifery and Women's Health, 52*(4), 323–333.

Gamble, J., & Creedy, D. (2009). Counseling model for postpartum women after distressing birth experiences. *Midwifery, 25*(2), e21–e30.

Gaskin, I. M. (1977/1990). *Spiritual midwifery* (3rd ed.). Summertown: The Book Publishing Company.

Geertz, C. (1973). *The interpretation of culture*. New York: Basic Books.

Goer, H., & Wheeler, R. (1999). *The thinking woman's guide to a better birth*. Pedigree Books.

Grajeda, R., Perez-Escamilla, R., & Dewey, K. (1997). Delayed clamping of the umbilical cord improves hematologic status of Guatemalan infants at 2 months of age. *The American Journal of Clinical Nutrition, 65*(2), 425–431.

Greenwood, D., Lindebaum, S., Lock, M., & Young, A. (1988). Introduction theme issue: Medical anthropology. *American Ethnologist 15*(1), 1–3.

Griesemer, L. M. (1998). *Unassisted homebirth: An act of love*. Charleston: Terra Publishing.

Gupta, J., & Hofmeyr, G. (2004). Position for women during second stage of labour. *Cochrane Database of Systematic Reviews, 1*: CD002006.

Gupta, R., & Ramji, S. (2002). Effect of delayed cord clamping on iron stores in infants born to anemic mothers: A randomized controlled trial. *Indian Pediatrics, 39*(2), 130–135.

Hamilton, J., & Lobel, M. (2008). Types, patterns, and predictors of coping with stress during pregnancy: Examination of the revised prenatal coping inventory in a diverse sample. *Journal of Psychosomatic Obstetrics and Gynecology, 29*(2), 97–104.

Harris, G. (2000). Homebirth and independent midwifery. *Australian College of Midwives Incorporated Journal, 13*(2), 10–16.

Hay, C. (2002). Childbirth in America: A historical perspective. In H. M. Sterk, K. Ratcliffe, C. H. Hay, A. B. Kehoe, & L. VandeVusse (Eds.), *Who's having this baby? Perspectives on birthing* (pp. 9–42). East Lansing: Michigan State University Press.

Hazard, C., Callister, L., Birkhead, A., & Nichols, L. (2009). Hispanic labor friends initiative: Supporting vulnerable women. *American Journal of Maternal Child Nursing, 34*(2), 115–121.

Higgens, D. L., & Metzler, M. (2001). Implementing community-based participatory research centers in diverse urban settings. *Journal of Urban Health, 38*(3), 488–494.

Hodnett, E. D., Gates, S., Hofmeyr, G. J., & Sakala, C. (2007). Continuous support for women during childbirth (Cochrane Review). *Cochrane Database of Systematic Reviews, 3*, 1–72.

Israel, B. J., Schulz, A. J., Parker, E. A., & Becker, A. B. (2001). Community-based participatory research: Policy recommendations for promoting a partnership approach in health research. *Education for Health, 14*(2), 182–197.

Janssen, P., Lee, S., Ryan, E., Etches, D., Farquharson, D., Peacock, D., & Klein, M. (2002). Outcomes of planned home births versus planned hospital births after regulation of midwifery in British Columbia. *Canadian Medical Association Journal, 166*(3), 315–323.

Janssen, P., Saxell, L., Page, L., Klein, M., Liston, R., & Lee, S. (2009). Outcomes of planned home birth with registered midwife versus planned hospital birth with midwife or physician. *Canadian Medical Association Journal, 181*(6–7), 377–383.

Johansen, O., Brox, J., & Flaten, M. (2003). Placebo and nocebo responses, cortisol, and circulating beta-endorphins. *Psychosomatic Medicine, 65*(5), 786–790.

Johnson, C. B., & Davis-Floyd, R. (2006). Home to hospital transport: Fractured articulations and magical mandorlas. In R. Davis-Floyd & C. B. Johnson (Eds.), *Mainstreaming midwives: The politics of change* (pp. 469–506). New York: Taylor and Francis Group.

Johnson, K. C., & Daviss, B. A. (2005). Outcomes of planned home births with certified professional midwives: Large prospective study in North America. *British Medical Journal, 330*(7505), 1416–1422.

Jolly, A. (1999). *Lucy's legacy: Sex and intelligence in human evolution.* Cambridge: Harvard University Press.

Jordan, B. (1978/1993). *Birth in four cultures: A crosscultural investigation of childbirth in Yucatan, Holland, Sweden and the United States* (4th ed.). Prospect Heights, IL: Waveland Press.

Klassen, P. (2001). *Blessed events: Religion and home birth in America.* Princeton: Princeton University Press.

Klein, M., Grzybowski, S., Harris, S., Liston, R., Spence, A., Le, G., Brummendorf, D., Kim, S., & Kaczorowski, J. (2001). Epidural analgesia use as a marker for physician approach to birth: Implication for maternal and newborn outcomes. *Birth, 28*(4), 243–248.

Konner, M., & Shostack, M. (1987). Timing and management of birth among the !Kung: Biocultural interaction in reproductive adaptation. *Cultural Anthropology, 2*(1), 11–28.

Krogman, W. (1951). The scars of human evolution. *Scientific American, 185,* 54–57.

Lawrence, A., Lewis, L., Hofmeyr, G. J., Dowswell, T., & Styles, C. (2009). Maternal positions and mobility during first stage labour. *Cochrane Database of Systematic Reviews, 2*: CD003934.

Lichtigfield, F., & Gillman, M. (2002). Possible role of the endogenous opioid system in the placebo response in depression. *The International Journal of Neuropsychopharmacology, 5*(1), 107–108.

Luce, J., & Pincus, J. (1998). Childbirth. In Boston Women's Health Book Collective (Ed.), *Our bodies, ourselves for the new century* (pp. 466–501). New York: Touchstone.

MacDorman, M., Declercq, E., Menacker, F., & Malloy, M. (2006). Infant and neonatal mortality for primary cesarean and vaginal births to women with "no indicated risk," United States, 1998–2001 birth cohorts. *Birth, 33*(3), 175–182.

Martin, J., Hamilton, B., Sutton, P., Ventura, S., Menacker, F., Kirmeyer, S., & Munson, M. (2009). Births: Final data for 2006. *National Vital Statistics Reports, 56*(6), 1–104.

McKinley, J. (1986). A case for refocusing upstream: The political economy of illness. In P. Conrad & R. Kerr (Eds.), *The sociology of health and illness* (pp. 613–633). New York: St. Martin's Press.

McRae, C., Cherin, E., Yamazaki, T. G., Diem, G., Vo, A. H., Russell, D., Heiner Ellgring, J., Fahn, S., Greene, P., Dillon, S., Winfield, H., Bjugstad, K. B., & Freed, C. R. (2004). Effects of perceived treatment on quality of life and medical outcomes in a double-blind placebo surgery trial. *Archives of General Psychiatry, 61,* 412–420.

Mercer, J. (2001). Current best evidence: A review of the literature on umbilical cord clamping. *Journal of Midwifery and Women's Health, 46*(6), 402–414.

Mercer, J., McGrath, M., Hensman, A., Silver, H., & Oh, W. (2003). Immediate and delayed cord clamping in infants born between 24 and 32 weeks: A pilot randomized controlled trial. *Journal of Perinatology, 23*(6), 466–472.

Mitford, J. (1992). *The American way of birth.* New York: Dutton.

Murphy, P. and J. Fullerton. 1998. Outcomes of Intended Home Births in Nurse-Midwifery Practice: A Prospective Descriptive Study. *Obstetrics and Gynecology 92*(3), 461–470.

Nash, J. (2007). Consuming interests: Water, rum, and Coca-Cola from ritual propitiation to corporate expropriation in Highland Chiapas. *Cultural Anthropology, 22*(4), 621–639.

Northam, S., & Knapp, T. R. (2006). The reliability and validity of birth certificates. *JOGNN, 35*(1), 3–12.

Northrup, C. (2002). *Women's bodies, women's wisdom.* New York: Bantam Books.

Oakley, A. (1984). *The captured womb: A history of the medical care of pregnant women.* Oxford: Basil Blackwell Publisher Ltd.

O'Connell, M., Hussain, J., Maclennan, F., & Lindow, S. (2003). Factors associated with a prolonged second state of labour - A case-controlled study of 364 nulliparous labours. *Journal of Obstetrics and Gynecology, 23*(3), 255–257.

O'Toole, T. P., Felix Aaron, K., Chin, M. H., Horowitz, C., & Tyson, F. (2003). Community-based participatory research: Opportunities, challenges and the need for a common language. *Journal of General and Internal Medicine, 18*, 592–594.

Oxorn, H. (1986). *Oxorn-Foote human labor and birth* (3rd ed.). New York: Appleton-Century-Crofts.

Paulson, S. (2006). Body, nation, and consubstantiation in Bolivian ritual meals. *American Ethnologist, 33*(4), 650–664.

Pollock, L. A. (1990). Embarking on a rough passage: The experience of pregnancy in early-modern society. In V. Fildes (Ed.), *Women as mothers in pre-industrial England* (pp. 39–67). London: Routledge.

Porter, R., & Porter, D. (1988). *In sickness and in health: The British experience 1650–1850.* London: Fourth Estate.

Rabe, H., Reynolds, G., & Diaz-Rossello, J. (2004). Early versus delayed umbilical cord clamping in preterm infants. *Cochrane Database of Systematic Reviews, 4*: CD003248.

Robins, S. (2006). From "rights" to "ritual": AIDS activism in South Africa. *American Anthropologist, 108*(2), 312–323.

Roelofs, J., ter Riet, G., Peters, M., Kessels, A., Reulen, J., & Menheere, P. (2000). Expectations of analgesia do not affect spinal nociceptive R-III reflex activity: An experimental study into the mechanism of placebo-induced analgesia. *Pain, 89*(1), 75–80.

Rosenberg, K. (1992). The evolution of modern human childbirth. *American Journal of Physical Anthropology, 35*, 89–124.

Rothman, B. K. (1982/1991). *In labor: Women and power in the birthplace.* New York: W.W. Norton and Company.

Rothman, B. K. (1987a). *The tentative pregnancy: Prenatal diagnosis and the future of motherhood.* New York: Penguin Books.

Rothman, B. K. (1987b). Reproductive technology and the commodification of life. *Women and Health, 13*(1–2), 95–100.

Runes, V. V. (Ed.). (2004). *From calling to courtroom: A survival guide for midwives.* IL: From Calling to Courtroom, Inc.

Salmon, P., & Drew, N. (1992). Multidimensional assessment of women's experience of childbirth: Relationship to obstetric procedure, antenatal preparation and obstetric history. *Journal of Psychosomatic Research, 36*(4), 317–327.

Save the Children. (2007). *State of the world's mothers.* Westport, CT: Author.

Scott, P. (2003). *Sit up and take notice!* New Zealand: Great Scott Publications.

Scott, P., & Sutton, J. (1996). *Understanding and Teaching Optimal Foetal Positioning.* Birth Concept, New Zealand.

Sher, L. (2004). The role of endogenous opioids in the placebo effect in post-traumatic stress disorder. *Forschende Komplementarmedizin und Klassische Naturheilkunde, 11*,(6), 354–359.

Shostack, M. (1981). *Nisa: The life and words of a !Kung woman.* Cambridge: Harvard University Press.

Simpson, K., & Atterbury, J. (2003). Trends and issues in labor induction in the United States: Implications for clinical practice. *Journal of Obstetrics, Gynecologic, and Neonatal Nursing, 32*(6), 767–779.

Singer, M. (1990). Reinventing medical anthropology: Toward a critical re-alignment. *Social Science and Medicine, 30*(2), 179–188.

Singer, M. (1995). Beyond the ivory tower: Critical praxis in medical anthropology. *Medical Anthropology Quarterly, 9*(1), 80–106.

Singer, M., Scott, G., Wilson, S., Easton, D., & Weeks, M. (2001). "War stories": AIDS prevention and the street narratives of drug users. *Qualitative Health Research, 11*(5), 589–611.

Stearns, S., Nesse, R., & Haig, D. (2008). Introducing evolutionary thinking for health and medicine. In S. Stearns & J. Koella (Eds.), *Evolution in health and disease* (pp. 1–16). Oxford: Oxford University Press.

To, W., & Li, I. (2000). Occipital posterior and occipital transverse positions: Reappraisal of the obstetric risks. *Australian and New Zealand Journal of Obstetrics and Gynaecology, 40,* 275–279.

Torvaldsen, S., Roberts, C., Bell, J., & Raynes-Greenow, C. (2004). Discontinuation of epidural analgesia late in labour for reducing the adverse delivery outcomes associated with epidural analgesia. *Cochrane Database of Systematic Reviews, 4:* CD004457.

Tracy, S., Sullivan, E., Wang, Y., Black, D., & Tracy, M. (2007). Birth outcomes associated with interventions in labour amongst low risk women: A population-based study. *Women and Birth, 20*(2), 41–48.

Trevathan, W. (1987). *Human birth: An evolutionary perspective.* New York: Aldine de Gruyter.

Trevathan, W. (1997). An evolutionary perspective on authoritative knowledge about birth. In R. Davis-Floyd & C. Sargent (Eds.), *Childbirth and authoritative knowledge* (pp. 80–90). Berkeley: University of California Press.

Trevathan, W. (1999). Evolutionary obstetrics. In W. Trevathan, E. O. Smith, & J. McKenna (Eds.), *Evolutionary medicine* (pp. 183–208). New York: Oxford Press.

Trevathan, W., Smith, E. O., & McKenna, J. (Eds.). (2008). *Evolutionary medicine and health: New perspectives.* New York: Oxford University Press.

Turner, V. (1969). *The ritual process: Structure and anti-structure.* Chicago: Aldine Publishing Company.

Turner, V. (1974). *Dramas, fields and metaphors: Symbolic action in human society.* Ithaca, NY: Cornell University Press.

Turner, V. (1977). Variations on a theme of liminality. In S. Moore & B. Myerhoff

(Eds.), *Secular ritual* (pp. 35–62). Assen, The Netherlands: Van Gorcum.

Turner, V. (1979). Betwixt and between: The liminal period in rites de passage. In W. Lessa & E. Z. Vogt (Eds.), *Reader in comparative religion: An anthropological approach* (4th ed., pp. 234–243). New York: Harper and Row.

Ulrich, L. T. (1990). *A midwife's tale*. New York: Vintage Books.

van Gennep, A. (1909/1960). *The rites of passage*. Chicago: University of Chicago Press.

van Rheenen, P., & Brabin, B. (2004). Late umbilical cord-clamping as an intervention for reducing iron deficiency anemia in term infants in developing and industrialised countries: A systematic review. *Annals of Tropical Paediatrics, 24*(1), 3–16.

Wagner, M. (2006). *Born in the USA: How a broken maternity system must be fixed to put mothers and babies first*. Berkeley: University of California Press.

Walker, J. (2000). Quality of midwifery care given throughout the world: Report of the Fourth International Homebirth Conference, Amsterdam. *Midwifery, 16*(2), 161–164.

Walrath, D. (2003). Rethinking pelvic typologies and the human birth mechanism. *Current Anthropology, 44*(1), 5–31.

Walrath, D. (2006). Gender, genes, and the evolution of human birth. In P. Geller & M. Stockett (Eds.), *Feminist anthropology: Past present and future*

(pp. 55–72). Philadelphia: University of Pennsylvania Press.

Wertz, R. W., & Wertz, D. C. (1977/1989). *Lying-in: A history of childbirth in America*. New York: Free Press.

Wickham, S. (2008). Unassisted birth: Listening and earning from the minority. *The Practising Midwife, 11*(6), 4–5.

Wiley, A., & Katz, S. (1998). Geophagy in pregnancy: A test of a hypothesis. *Current Anthropology, 39*, 532–545.

Wirtz, K. (2007). *Ritual, discourse, and community in Cuban Santería: Speaking a sacred world*. Gainesville: University Press of Florida.

World Health Organization (WHO). (2004). *Numbers: Review of maternal deaths and complications to make pregnancy safer*. Geneva, Switzerland: Author.

World Health Organization (WHO). (2007). *Neonatal and perinatal mortality: Country, regional and global estimates 2004*. Geneva, Switzerland: Author.

Zachariah, R. (2009). Social support, life stress, and anxiety as predictors of pregnancy complications in low-income women. *Research in Nursing and Health, 32*(4), 391–404.

Zhang, J., Troendle, J., & Yancy, M. (2002). Reassessing the labor curve in nulliparous women. *American Journal of Obstetrics and Gynecology, 187*(4), 824–828.

Index

Note: Page numbers with t refer to Tables